Don't miss any of Kevin Russell's

Dad's & Mom's Do's & Don'ts Series

Dad's & Mom's Disney Do's & Don'ts

Dad's & Mom's Internet Safety Do's & Don'ts

Dad's (& Mom's) Internet Safety Do's & Don'ts

INTERNET SAFETY ADVICE WRITTEN BY DAD, APPROVED BY MOM, AND UNNOTICED BY OUR KIDS

By Kevin Russell

Copyright

Dad's & Mom's Internet Safety Do's & Don'ts
Copyright © 2015 by Kevin Russell
All rights reserved.

Inquiries should be addressed to:
The Russell Center, LLC
7202 Giles Road
Suite 4, Mail Stop #200
La Vista NE 68128

SECOND EDITION
First Printing (2015)

Russell, Kevin

Dad's & Mom's Internet Safety Do's & Don'ts: Internet Safety Advice Written by Dad approved by Mom, Unnoticed by our children

ISBN-10:0985226560
ISBN-13:978-0-9852265-6-5

Printed in the United States of America
By The Russell Center, LLC
http://www.dadsdosanddonts.com

Dedication

For Spike, my favorite furry little avatar.

This book is inspired by the teens from PCCYG. Yeah, you're adults now, but I still pray you'll be safe out there!
I also need to thank my wife and kids. They are the guinea pigs for most of the security stuff that I have put in this book … and a few things that didn't make it. They put up with a lot.

-Kevin

Preface

I spend my days working in the world of information security. I watch companies large and small make simple mistakes that lead to large issues. Watching these companies makes me see how my family and friends are much less protected than these companies with teams of people running robust security departments. I see how vulnerable the teens in my church's youth group are because of their online behavior. What started as nagging these kids every Sunday night in my role as youth group leader has exploded into full blown lectures around the Midwest at churches, schools, and public libraries to try to offer some knowledge to people who have to live with the Internet. The lectures expanded, a handout was created, and then a blog was set up. The message of safety, security, and privacy for families is too important to be reserved for the corporate world. And so this book is born. In these pages I tell stories, offer suggestions, and spread knowledge that every person and parent needs to help keep themselves and their family safe. I hope you enjoy the book, its stories, and its message.

Check out my blog at www.dadsinternetsafety.blogspot.com

Contents

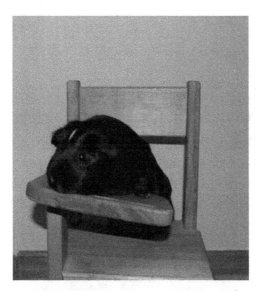

INTRODUCTION or "Why Am I a Guinea Pig?"

YOU MIGHT BE WONDERING WHY there is a picture of a super adorable guinea pig on the cover of this book. You may also be wondering why I dedicated my book to Spike. The story begins like this:

SPIKE WAS MY DAUGHTER'S "RESCUE PIG". We adopted him at the Humane Society where he was on his second go-round. After about two weeks, when it became apparent that the cleaning of Spike's pen would become my duty, he rapidly became my best friend. To my daughter's complete horror, I taught Spike to head-butt me on command and to squeak when I called him "Dude".

A few years into his membership in our family, I got home from work and logged onto my Facebook account with an audience of children snickering and hovering behind me, not completely uncommon behavior for my children, but a little odd. I checked my home page, checked on my pirates, and headed for my favorite game. They looked disappointed and wandered off.

Sitting at the computer next to mine, my wife pointed to her screen and said, "Congrats. You got you 100k badge." I leaned over and saw (along with my coveted 100K badge) my daughter's guinea pig looking at me from a little picture with my name under it. After a moment of confusion, I realized what I was seeing. I clicked "profile" and, sure enough, instead of my blank picture (yes, I did not post one) was a picture of our little black guinea pig patiently sitting in a doll's school desk. Both my girls and my wife burst out laughing as I realized, "HEY, I am a guinea pig!"

Long story, but it has a point. How did I become a guinea pig? Well, I shared my password. Why would I, the paranoid security dude, do that? That story is for another chapter... But the lesson here for kids and adults alike is: *When other people know your passwords, you become a guinea pig, or worse*. This story is only cute, but if my pre-teen password pirates had wanted to, they could have changed many settings – including the password - and "taken over" my account.

I am actually not a guinea pig. No, really, I am not. What I am is an information security professional, father, and involved parent who has become concerned with my family's safety on the Internet. In my business life I am a risk and security professional and have a number of certifications including certified information systems security professional (CISSP) and certified in risk and information systems control (CRISC). I help businesses design, establish, and evaluate security and risk programs.

I spent several years as the co-director of our church high school youth group. Those amazing young people taught me a great deal. One of the lessons was, "Even very smart kids need advice to be safe on the Internet". Parents fight an uphill battle to stay level with their kids on the latest Internet, social media, and communication vehicles. I started lecturing to youth groups, schools and eventually touring school districts in the Midwest to spread the message of Internet safety to youth and their parents. At least once a year, I work with our local library to offer an Internet safety course. From these sessions I started to recognize a pattern of questions, mainly from parents and grandparents. My handouts grew. I finally decided to compile all of my presentations into this book. Hopefully, this information will help you to keep your family and your kids safe on the Internet.

This book was written to arm you (parents, grandparents, teachers, youth group leaders, and any other concerned adults) with enough knowledge about the perils and pitfalls of the Internet so you can help to keep children safe and yourself current. The strategies outlined in this book are a lot like the sweater and sunscreen we use to equip our children to prepare for the elements. My wife and I have tried these on our own children (and some I have tried on my professional clients). We hope to help you safeguard your children with a minimum of hassles. To over-extend the sweater/sunscreen analogy, we've learned that when you force your child to wear a sweater to the pool, you get less than optimal results... and you annoy the child. The do's and don'ts that we've compiled may help you avoid using tools that are more expensive than you require, overkill for the job you're trying to do, or just plain wrong and won't give your family the protection that they need.

Throughout the book (usually at the end of each chapter), you will find advice in the form of Do's and Don'ts, summarizing strategies to help keep your child – and family – a safer on the Internet. Ranging from do-it-yourself basics to more technical instructions, these concepts fall into three categories or, as I like to call them, the

"Top Three Do's and Don'ts for Parents":

1. **Do**: Stay involved. Setting your family up to safely explore the Internet is not a one-time, turn-key operation. By making the Internet a family event and working with your kids, side-by-side, parents can set Internet rules, and model good Internet behaviors. Ultimately, parents need to know and watch for warning signs that

children may be straying into dangerous territory (like when the browser has no history or kids close the laptop or quickly click the mouse key when you walk in).

2. **Don't**: Do NOT share! This seems opposite to what we've been teaching our kids since they were out of their cribs, but the path to Internet disaster is lined with good intentions and over-sharing. Children need to know that sharing passwords is not okay. Parents need to know how to keep from accidentally sharing their wireless networks. Everyone needs to know the critical dangers of sharing too much information on their social media sites.

3. **Do**: Set up a safe environment. Tons of tools are available to ensure your family's safe use of the Internet. One key piece of equipment that you'll need can actually be held in your hands: a router that can protect your family with a firewall. You'll also need reputable software for antivirus, child protection, activity monitoring, and more in-depth internet security services.

DO: STAY INVOLVED

Screen Time or 'Unnoticed by Our Kids'

When I see parents nowadays the most often asked question is:
"How do I keep the kids safe on the internet?"
and the second one is:
"How much time should I allow them to be on the computer?"
When you are done, I will just hand them the book with all of the answers.

WHILE I WAS WRITING THIS BOOK, a clinical psychologist with a reputation distinctive for working with children contacted me with the top two questions she hears from parents on the topics of: (1) Internet safety and (2) computer time. We're hoping to address the first question through the strategies offered throughout this book to help keep children safe on the Internet, but that's an answer that will take at least a hundred pages. We can, however, tackle the sticky problem of computer time right here and now.

It's difficult to find expert recommendations for limiting children's Internet time. Much more research pertains to kids watching television than to kids spending time on the Internet or computer. This is probably because parents have had more years to worry about the TV. The American

Academy of Pediatrics has posted recommendations for children's "screen time" – screen time here encompasses TV, movies, video and computer games – to <u>no more than one or two hours a day</u>. The consequences of more than two hours of daily screen time are bad. Some are very bad.

The Mayo Clinic links too much screen time (not just TV time, but the full gamut of screens) to:

★ Obesity
★ Poor sleep habits
★ Emotional, social and attention problems
★ Deterioration of academic performance
★ Desensitization to violence
★ Less time for creative, active play (at our house we call a game like computer solitaire a "TIME SUCK".)

Now that we know how much screen time is inappropriate, how do we limit screen time to appropriate amounts? This is a topic that many, many parenting blogs have fearlessly championed. My favorite advice from them was "be a parent". Very helpful. A list from the Mayo Clinic suggests some basics that may enhance the "be a parent" gem. I paraphrase a few below:

★ Turn off the TV when it's just serving as background noise
★ No screens in the bedroom (no TV, DVR, computer, game console, or internet-connected phones)
★ No eating in front of the TV
★ Set house rules for screen time during the school week
★ Make sure your child's caregivers enforce these rules, too
★ Suggest other activities
★ Be a good role model
★ Unplug it - the context is to unplug when "screen time is becoming a source of tension in your family". (Suggestions include designating one day each week as "screen-free" or even putting a lock on your TV's electrical plug to prevent kids from circumventing your unplugged mandate.)

These are a fair reflection of how we handle screen time at our house, with the exception of setting a rule limiting screen time. When we observe that screen time is taking over other areas of our children's lives, we tend to be a little less confrontational. In keeping with the criteria that we developed for this book – *Advice Written by Dad, Approved by Mom, and Unnoticed by Our Kids* – we rely more on redirection. Should a child be observed to be in danger of becoming one with the keyboard, the dog suddenly needs a trip to the pet store that requires the "pet owner's" assistance; or the pleasure of our children's company is requested for loading the dishwasher; or a nature walk spontaneously breaks out involving the zoo or local forest center. You get the picture – we usually develop a fun alternative. If their behavior has become annoying or we are out of coffee, sometimes we are not as creative and chores become our source of redirection.

Another suggestion from Mayo Clinic may allow you to look like a hero in your child's eyes: charge the phone overnight in a room other than the child's bedroom. I would introduce this after your child has let her phone go dead a couple of times. Now you can become the helpful parent by setting up a charging station in your bedroom. Each night before bed, remind your child that it's time to charge her phone (and any other portable electronic devices), gather the items at your charging station, and tuck your child into bed.

Wait. Aren't we eliminating an opportunity to teach our child responsibility for charging the phone? Lessons with natural consequences like "forget to charge your phone and you'll have no power" are few and far between. Phooey. Our goal here is to maintain control of the Internet-accessing devices. By overnighting them in a place other than your child's bedroom, you now have assurances that they are not up all night texting, tweeting, emailing, and posting. As a bonus, your child likely won't notice this strategy until he is a teenager.

I can assure you, however, that the one time we engaged the Mayo Clinic's "unplug it" strategy, in response to the most heinous crime of talking back to their very sweet piano teacher, I believe our kids did notice.

Danger Signs or 'Worst Case Scenarios'

I AM NOT GOING TO TELL YOU what the Internet is or its history. Most people think of the Internet as a search engine. Almost everyone interacts with it at least once a day. The fact that "googling" something has actually become a word in our language speaks to the omnipresent power of the Internet. Whether checking email at work, looking up a movie start time, or buying a toaster online, we all deal with the Internet continuously. You can access it with your phone, your computer, your gaming consoles, your television, your iPod/iPad/tablet and your eBook reader.

The Internet is a great source of information. Most of that information is worthwhile and accurate. Some is not. Now imagine the worst thing you can. What you just imagined can be found on the Internet, in great and graphic detail. The search could have been on purpose or an accident, but the results are just as horrific. I am not telling you that your child will be scarred for life because they saw something unpleasant or inappropriate in a search return, but, if you are present when that happens then you can react to it and mitigate any damage.

As you probably know, the Internet has no filter. When my wife and daughter began to search for information about the book "Moby Dick" by Herman Melville, they had some search results that could have been interpreted as offensive by many. Certainly by us. Ewwww. Thankfully, my wife was working with my daughter on this and was able to use this as a teaching moment.

The Internet invites dozens of these "teaching moments" into our homes every day. As parents we remind our children to put on a sweater or sunscreen, depending on the circumstances. How did we learn to nag our children about these dangers? When we were children we were nagged by our parents, who were nagged by theirs… But the Internet is so new and changing so quickly that we have no source of sage, time-tested advice. In fact, by the time advice has been expertly tested, not only have the rules changed, but our kids are playing an entirely different game. Parents need a baseline of knowledge that they can use to adapt to the constantly evolving environment of the Internet, because with or without a sweater, on the Internet, our children are vulnerable to predators that can rob them of their money, self-respect, or even their lives.

These predators actively set traps that can expose our children to hazards like:

★ Stranger danger,
★ Cyberbullying,
★ Identity theft,
★ Computer viruses, and
★ Pornography .

My first and best advice for parents is to start your child's time on the Internet early and with you. Work with your children from an early age and make Internet time like any other form of family entertainment time. Together time allows you to teach your child to be safe on the Internet. You can turn those "oops" moments into learning opportunities.

That Moby Dick story was a great "Oops" moment that my wife used with our daughter to teach her about what happens when you search the

Internet. Why did they get results like those even in Safe Search mode? Nothing is perfect, and some of the results used the second word of the title and returned "medical advice" about that piece of anatomy. She showed my daughter to put "Moby Dick" in quotes and use correct caps to get a cleaner search return.

In our house the computers that we use for the Internet are together in our computer room (really, in our dining room which is filled with desks and computers instead of dining furniture, but "computer room" sounds cooler). My wife and I use our computers in that room when we are not at work. If our children want to be on the web or use the Internet for homework, they work in the same room. This way we can keep an eye on what is going on. We own a couple of tablets. Those are used in many rooms, but only one with an adult in it. One place we finally eased off is our eldest's phone Internet use. She is in high school now, and we treat her like a person who has been taught the best way to behave on the Internet. That does not mean she gets free rein. Nope. My wife regularly asks for the phone and reviews text messages and browser history… just to keep her on her toes. See _Reviewing Your Child's Browser History_ .

My wife and I have rules for computer use, the Internet, and social media. Our rules for social media require that our children's first friends are Mom and Dad. This way, we get to see everything that they post. We also require them to share their passwords with us, so we can check settings and other items regularly. We do. We read email. We look at Facebook. And we look at their phones. We try hard to keep this positive, and so far it is working, probably because we are quite transparent about it. We take the phone, read it, and hand it back. No "spying", "sneaking", or "prying". Hopefully, they feel protected.

When your child starts getting older, you still need to pay more attention to the way that they use the Internet. Does your youth disappear and ONLY work on the computer when you are NOT around? I head this off by not allowing computers in their rooms. Additional assistance is available through devices and software. We address these in detail in "_Setting up Your Home Network_." Most routers offer parental controls of some kind. These can set hours of use and require user ids with passwords to track who is on the computer. There are software packages that you can purchase (or get for free …see K9) that can also set schedules and block periods of time.

Does your child shut off the screen or quickly close the laptop every time you walk past? Do they quickly change windows or react in an unusual way? This would make me take a look at what they are doing.

Kids are smart. They learn to hide what they are doing from parents. They work with computers at school. They learn from friends. Even if you don't see the most common red flags like quickly changing screens or closing the lid, they can still be hiding what they are doing. Our local newspaper ran a story that stated that more than 70% of all kids polled are hiding their Internet actions from their parents. The most common way was to clear the browser's history. For detailed information on how to read and secure browsers histories so they can't be erased, see *Configuration for a System for Kids* under *Setting Up a Safe Environment*.

The Internet can be a source of great pain and humiliation. Parents are terrified that their son or daughter will come home from school, get on their social media account, and find out that they have become the butt of a school-wide joke. How they react can be a worst case scenario. The computer and the Internet should be places of learning and wonder, not fear and loathing.

Pay attention to any warning signs or changes in behavior. The signs are similar to all of the drug information that you received from school. Watch for references to violence or self-harm. The National Institute for Mental Health mentions a few of the warning signs that may preclude suicide:

★ Feelings of hopelessness or worthlessness, depressed mood, poor self-esteem or guilt
★ Not wanting to participate in family or social activities
★ Changes in sleeping and eating patterns: too much or too little
★ Feelings of anger, rage, need for revenge
★ Feeling exhausted most of the time
★ Trouble with concentration, problems academically or socially in school
★ Feeling listless, irritable

* Regular and frequent crying
* Not taking care of yourself
* Reckless, impulsive behaviors
* Frequent physical symptoms such as headaches or stomach aches

If you have any questions, seek professional help sooner rather than later. You can talk to your local police department, or many schools have councilors who can point parents to resources. You can seek advice at your church, and the National Institute for Mental Health recommends a toll-free, 24-hour crisis line (1-800-273-TALK (8255)); see also http://www.suicidepreventionlifeline.org.

My wife has "friended" our children's friends on various social media sites, including Facebook, Twitter and Pinterest, among others. This way she can see what they are up to and give them kudos the next time she sees them in person. She is also looking for signs of danger. One day she read a few posts from a young adult that worried her. He sounded like he was considering suicide. She immediately contacted the friend's mother who was able to connect him to the help that he needed. These warnings are not restricted to teens, and we should all be aware of these signs every time we are on a social media site.

The FBI created a profile of the youth who shot their fellow students at Columbine High School. The profile has fit virtually every other youth who has done something similar since then. In every case there was a message on a social media site that would have served as a clue to professionals. In the last year, law enforcement has stopped a number of school shootings before they happened because either a fellow student or parent saw the clues and told someone.

Talk to your kids about how to watch for messages that sound dangerous. Tell them to contact an adult immediately.

Cyberbullying

Cyberbullying is soaring problem. The term "cyberbullying" is normally reserved for youth and "cyber harassment" is usually used for adults. In the old days, when I went to school, a bully had to bully someone in person. Anonymous bullying was almost impossible. Today that is not the case. Kids can create a fake Facebook account and post anything they want on someone's wall. They can take a humiliating video in class on their cell phone and post it on YouTube. The whole landscape of bullying has changed dramatically. It is easy for people of any age to say mean and hurtful things about anyone at any time. There are anonymous blogs that do nothing but spew malicious information. People post mean pictures on social media pages all of the time. This new form of bullying can be even more damaging than the physical kind. In fact, this form of bullying can and does lead to the same problems as bullying in person, except it is harder for us as parents to see that it is happening.

Talk to your children. There are many great websites full of information about cyberbullying. Virtually all agree that you need to talk to your kids before it happens and tell them to report it. MTV has a fantastic site to educate and help youth get assistance and protection from cyberbullying. The site is www.thethinline.org. Visit it and learn how you can educate your children. Other resources include:

- ★ www.stopcyberbullying.org by the team at www.wiredsafety.org,
- ★ www.npc.org/cyberbullying, and
- ★ a government site at www.stopbullying.gov.

You can teach your children to block people whom they do not wish to interact with on almost all social media and email sites. If someone is bullying or harassing your child online, block them. By doing this, they can no longer see your child's posts, and your child can no longer see theirs. In Facebook you can "un-friend" someone as well as block them. On all sites you can search for help on "blocking". Facebook allows blocking in the accounts setting menus. Our advice for *Facebook blocking* is detailed in the *Set*

Up Instructions section. Twitter, Google+, and email systems let you block people by their email address, stop them from following you in Twitter by removing them from your followers, or even add their email address to your email system blocking list. Most of these sites also allow you to report inappropriate activity, which includes bullying.

When someone is blocked, they can still post anything they want about you or your child on their page, but you no longer see it. This may not solve a bullying problem. If your child is being bullied, talk to the authorities.

Schools are beginning to take cyberbullying seriously and treating it the same way as regular bullying. This excerpt from a high school handout describes what cyberbullying is and documents penalties for cyberbullying up to and including expulsion.

> *"Cyberbullying includes, but is not limited to, the following misuses of technology: harassing, teasing, intimidating, threatening, or terrorizing another person by sending or posting inappropriate and hurtful email messages, text messages, digital pictures or images, or Web site postings including blogs.*
>
> *Students or staff who feel that they have been the victim of such misuses of technology should not erase the offending material from the system. They should print a copy of the material and immediately report the incident to a school official. All reports of harassment in cyberspace will be investigated fully. Consequences for engaging in this type of misconduct may include, but are not limited to, the loss of computer privileges, confiscation of cell phones, detention, suspension, or expulsion from school. Law enforcement may also be contacted and involved."*

Predators

The Internet is full of predators. Please, talk to your children about the danger that these creeps pose. Regularly check your child's friends list. Our rule is that our children can only accept friends that I could meet and shake hands with. That doesn't mean I must shake their hand, but we have a tangible criteria that they must meet:

- ★ Do they go to your school?
- ★ Could you point them out to me at the next choir concert?
- ★ Are they at our church?
- ★ How do we know them?

When our children were younger, they wanted friends to play Webkinz games on-line. Our rule was even more concrete: You can only "friend" someone who has been in our house and pet our cat. Our poor kitty hid under the bed for a month.

Predators on the Internet will pose as girls (usually) who are about the same age as your child. They will look at as much "public" information as they can gather on your child, and then ask to be their friend. If your child accepts, they work to first gain their confidence, and then move on to more dangerous activities.

Make sure your child knows that they should NEVER meet anyone from an Internet site.

My friend had an embarrassing situation with her boy's promiscuous friending policy. To increase his number of friends (kids get competitive here), he accepted friend requests from a multitude of scantily clad, nubile young women who worked at Nevada houses of ill repute. Whenever these women posted their "marketing", it was broadcast across all of his friends' Facebook walls... Predators, or just marketers farming future customers? I'll let you decide.

Games or 'Put Down the Mouse!'

SOMETIMES THE PREDATOR is your child's self-control… or yours! My wife and I enjoy online games like World of Warcraft and Star Wars: The Old Republic. Our game computers sit in our computer room next to our kids' computers. One weekend after installing a new game, my wife and I got "sorta" hooked on it. After about eight hours, our daughter, munching on an inexpertly assembled peanut butter and jelly sandwich, entered the computer room and asked, "Are you going to make dinner today?" Apparently, even adults get hooked on games and need to be limited.

Online games are like social media. Within most of these games your child can chat with people, add friends, create a persona, and generally socialize with people from all over the world. In our house the same rules apply to games as to any social media site. If we are going to feel safe about our daughter playing the game, the rules are:

★ Our kids can add friends if they had been to our house and pet our cat.
★ We need to monitor what they are doing.
★ We must know who they are chatting to.

★ My wife and I must examine how the game works.

Our love for online games led us to purchasing accounts for our girls and playing together as a family. They got to play the game; we got to play the game; we got to know exactly who they were communicating with; and they got to learn how to make sandwiches.

Video console games and computer games often connect to the Internet. Treat them the same as a computer and follow the advice in this book about passwords, sharing accounts, scams, and your financial information. In the last year, two major game networks were hacked. In both cases, account data was stolen including user name, password, and credit card information. The safest thing to do is to treat a connected game like you would any website: think before you type.

Most games have filters that parents can set to block coarse language. Some have filters that will set time limits, and others have settings to identify your child's account as a minor's.

Do: Take the time to sit with your child while you install the game on their computer.

Do: Walk through the startup and account creation settings with them.

Do: Visit the menus in the game for all of the settings offered to protect your child.

Do: Look for "help communities" online that can assist you with making the best and safest settings in your child's account.

Do: Once you have set up the game, play it with your child for a while and make sure you understand how it works.

Do: Play to verify that the filters that you set appear to be working.

Don't: If your child is old enough, you can let them play on their own. Don't let them take the computer to their room to play.

Do: Check back every so often and play the game with them again to see that things are still the way you wish them to be.

Another gaming trap is addiction. Our girls and their friends used to play a game called VMK. It was created by Disney, was designed for kids, and incorporated many child protection features. We, as parents, liked the protections and found the game to be a safe and amusing place for our kids to play.

Our girls really liked the game. They played every moment that we allowed. They connected with their school friends in the game and played together. It was great, until Disney shut it down! Then our house descended into sadness and mourning. Our girls went into withdrawals. We thought about finding a methadone clinic for them. It was amazing. I had no idea a game could be so addicting to kids.

In doing some research on this topic, my wife found a study by the American Academy of Pediatrics that identified 9% of the children in the study as "gaming excessively". The study also showed that boys were much more likely to have an addiction to video games than girls. Children with "excessive gaming" had higher levels of depression and other mental health issues than their peers who played fewer games and for fewer hours. This study is not just about computer games. Video games, whether on a console (Xbox, PS3, Nintendo Wii) or a computer, are equally compelling when it comes to addiction.

Symptoms of Addiction to Video Games

The Center for Online Addiction published this list of warning signs for parents:

★ Playing for increasing amounts of time (most free time spent online)
★ Thinking about gaming during other activities (even dropping other activities that they used to love, falling behind at school, or not turning in their homework)
★ Gaming to escape from real-life problems, anxiety, or depression
★ Lying to friends and family to conceal gaming (aggressively protecting gaming privileges)
★ Feeling irritable when trying to cut down on gaming (withdrawal symptoms)

If you see these signs or are worried about your child, don't ignore them. Professionals recommend keeping a log of their game time. Document:

★ when your child plays and for how long
★ problems resulting from gaming, and
★ how the child reacts to time limits.

Seek professional help. Talk to your doctor, school counselor, church or the National Institute for Mental Health's 24-hour crisis line. They all can point you to the help you need.

National Institute for Mental Health recommends a toll-free, 24-hour crisis line (1-800-273-TALK (8255).

Monitoring or 'Quit Spying On Me!'

A GOOD FRIEND HAD A VERY INTERESTING SITUATION. His son, who had been living with the above rules since the day he was allowed his first email account, was fine with them until he got a girlfriend. But he didn't complain. He changed the rules. He used his school email account to acquire a free email account and began using it. He started having "phone problems" where the phone mysteriously didn't have any call history or text messages. My friend, a computer security professional as well, began to suspect his son was also hiding his Internet activities.

One day when he finished making dinner, he called his family to dinner and his son yelled out "Just a moment, I am finishing an email."

At the dinner table, his wife asked the son, "Did you see the email I forwarded to you with the schedule for band?"

"No."

Dinner ended and my friend was becoming more suspicious. "Hey son, who were you emailing just before dinner?"

"Jessica" was the immediate answer.

My friend went to his office after dinner and signed onto his son's email account. He found that his son had not emailed Jessica in three months and had not even opened any email in almost a month. His "spidey senses" were now tingling at full speed. He poked his head into his son's room and saw he was on the computer typing away. He went back to his office and looked at the router's logs. His son's computer was not on the network.

Uh oh! Another set of tingles. He shut off the wireless and went back to his son's room.

"Hey son, what are you doing?"

"Homework" answered his son, rotating the laptop so his dad could see the screen where the schools own search engine was displayed.

"Really?" asked my friend. "How?"

His son looked confused. "What do you mean?"

"Are you searching right now?" asked my friend.

"Yes," his son answered hitting the enter key. Sure enough the screen refreshed and the results were posted.

"I see," said my friend "That is strange. I disabled the network 10 minutes ago."

His son blanched and Dad took the computer.

His son had been using the neighbor's wireless network. The history on his browser showed that he had a secret free email account and had been browsing to places that were blocked at his home. Needless to say, he was in trouble.

This could happen to any parent who is not paying attention. Because my friend was a security professional, he was able to assemble the clues of missing information into a picture of misuse. He was able to review information on accounts and his own network devices. If you learn how to read your son's email, you will see when the account is not being used. If you learn how to read the usage reports on your network devices, you will see if your son is either misusing or not using your network.

Be prepared for the eye rolling or even name calling whenever you access your teen's information. But if you listen carefully you can hear the same names being yelled at all the parents in your neighborhood, sometimes just for doing a kid's laundry. This is the same thing as finding incriminating evidence in your child's pocket when you pull their blue jeans out of the dryer. By reading the notes you find in their pants, their email, their social media account, the call log on their phone, and their text messages, you are being the best parent you can be. Eventually you will have read enough email and looked at enough text messages that you will be glad you aren't in high school again yourself.

It may be comforting to know, as your child is accusing you of being the only parent who is so strict, that your child is just plain wrong. You are not the only concerned parent; you are actually in the majority. A 2010 survey by the Pew Research Center revealed that 64% of parents look at the contents of their child's cell phone. If this doesn't impress your child, perhaps this statistic (from the same survey) will: 62% of parents have taken away their child's phone as punishment.

If you are still afraid that your child's eyes will get stuck in the back of her head, you may want to reassure her that the interruptions will be less frequent once you are completely comfortable that she no longer requires that level of monitoring.

When is it time to loosen the Internet apron strings? Email can be tricky for parents. There is no set age requirement at many email providers. The choice is up to you and is based on your judgment of your child's maturity level. Email can be dangerous. Some spam is really inappropriate for children to read. We keep careful watch on our child's contact list. It is a good idea when they are younger to read their email always. As they get older, you can move to spot-checking their email. Don't forget to check the "deleted mail" or "Trash" folder, to see what your older youth has deleted to hide from you.

Don't: A child should NOT have her own email address until she is old enough to understand the dangers of email.

Do: Keep track of whoever your child communicates with.

Do: Watch accounts for spam that may be harmful.

Do: Work with your kids on their email and help them learn to identify and delete spam.

Do: Make use of the resources like the kids' settings for AOL www.kids.aol.com), Yahoo Kids (at www.kids.yahoo.com), and others that allow parents to set up "child" email accounts with tighter spam blocking and filtering.

Do: Most social media sites won't allow anyone under the age of 13 to have an account. But when they are old enough, and you let them have an account, you should sign up yourself (if you don't already have an account) and use it right along with them. Using social media together is fun and is a great way for you to monitor their activity.

Do: Read their posts.

Do: Be their friend.

Do: Make sure they keep their profile clear.

Do: Make them get your permission before posting any pictures. This particularly applies to Instagram, but our rule is for anything that leaves our house, be it via text, email, or social media. We really annoyed our daughter with this one. When you review pictures, remember to also look at the other kids in them and ask if your child has their permission to post pictures of them. If she treats the photos of her friends with respect, then she will come to expect that from her friends in return. If you see a post that is questionable, talk about it.

If you are worried your child is doing something unsafe, there are software products that capture and record all email and web activity. These are covered in _Tools for Safe Internet with Kids_.

Tools for Monitoring Your Children

Reviewing Your Child's Browser History

One of the most effective ways parents can monitor their children's activity on the Internet is sitting with them while they browse. As your child gets older, he will want to work on the Internet alone. When you start letting him use the Internet by himself, you should begin checking the browser history on the computer. Each of the big three browsers (Chrome™, Firefox™, and Internet Explorer™) have a method of reviewing the browsing history. This is a task you should do regularly. Be aware of the danger sign of a blank or very short history. This means someone has erased it and may be trying to hide something. Detailed instructions for reviewing browser history are found in *Browser History Review* in the Set Up Instructions.

In Pinterest you should follow your children's pins. First you can see their quantity of pins and make an educated guess as to the amount of time they are spending on the application; and, two, you can watch what they are pinning and "re-pinning" to make sure they remain appropriate.

Of additional note is the popular service Tumblr. There is no easy way to control Tumblr. Tumblr is a blog service that posts everything you (or your child!) posts immediately for the world to see. Tumblr requires only that the viewer be a registered member. You should check your child's browser history for *.tumblr.* to see if they are using this service and advise them on how to use it safely.

Tools for Facebook Monitoring

There is a collection of tools out there to help you monitor your child on Facebook and look for the signs of cyberbullying, inappropriate communication, dangerous friends, and drugs. Parents normally don't even need a Facebook account to get reports with these tools, although I still strongly recommend you set up a Facebook account and be your child's first friend. This gives you a front seat to watch all the action on their account from your account. This leads us to a great story about a kid and her "involved" parent.

One day my daughter entered the room and said, "My friend is so bored that she just posted a picture of herself sitting on top of the refrigerator." My wife and I couldn't resist signing into Facebook. Sure enough, there was my daughter's friend perched atop the refrigerator. We laughed. Then my wife pointed to the third comment down where a post from her father. Shouted, "<insert girls name here> Get off the fridge! I mean it, right now!" We laughed even harder. This is a fantastic example of an "involved" parent who made himself his kid's first Facebook friend and actually watches what his child posts. Kudos! An added benefit is that he may have just saved himself the cost of a new fridge and a new kid!

Tools range in price from free (like Minor Monitor) to inexpensive (like Trend Micro's Online Guardian, AVG Family Safety, and ZoneAlarm's SocialGuard). They all watch for key words in a youth's Facebook activity. They also examine friends and look for warning signs that a friend is not of their represented age (an adult posing as a friend). They look for a friend with few friends (a common characteristic of fake accounts). Grandmothers fit this profile too, so be careful who you block!

I really like Minor Monitor (www.minormonitor.com) for a child using Facebook and/or Twitter. This free tool watches not only for issues with your child, but with all of their friends. It will email you immediately if there is an event, but to access the normal monthly report, Minor Monitor requires you to log on to your account.

Every month we receive a report from AOL on our daughter's activity. You can see in the report in *Figure 1* that AOL summarizes the number of emails received and sent, the number of IMs received and sent, and the number of "forbidden" websites she tried to visit. By the report below you can tell she does not use her email account much. She usually texts her friends on her phone. A few months ago, the email summary showed 2 received and 334 sent. When my wife saw 334 emails sent, she knew we had a problem. Our daughter's account had been hacked. A "spammer" was using her account and her contact list to send spam. Her aunt had already received 5 emails from her highly recommending a certain men's medication that our 10-year-old daughter really should have had no knowledge of. Because her aunt had just deleted the emails, we would have never discovered the hack. The daily report from AOL proved invaluable. We called AOL, and they walked us through fixing the situation.

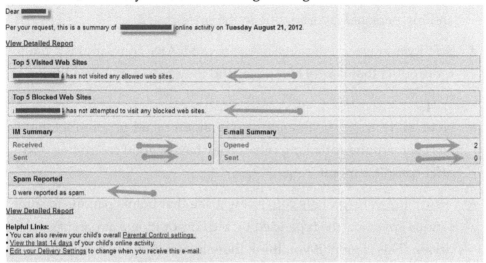

Figure 1: AOL Parents Monthly Report

Tools for Internet Safety with Kids

There are many tools parents can use to help protect their children and themselves on the Internet. My favorite tools for kids' email are:

★ Kids on AOL - Great child safety and control features - www..aol.com providesparental controls set and allows the account to be set to "kids" mode.

★ Yahoo Kids – more safe places for kids to go on the Internet – kids. yahoo.com

Web Content Control Software

My favorite web "content control" software is available for you to install directly onto your child's computer.

* K9 – by Blue Coat (www.getk9.com) is a GREAT free web filtering and my personal favorite (due to the price).

* Safe Eyes at www.internetsafety.com (a McAfee company) is a paid-for product that is very complete, and they have a mobile addition as well!

* Net Nanny at www.netnanny.com is another paid-for product that has been around for a long time. They have a good reputation and offer complete monitoring.

* www.Software4parents.com is a website that points parents to some serious spyware (the type used by big corporations) at parent's prices. This is great if you think there is something to be worried about, but is probably overkill for most households. This is serious corporate-level spyware you can install to monitor your child. Be aware that it requires that the child and you have separate computers.

* AVG Family Safety is also a complete PC-based monitoring solution – free.avg.com/us-en/avg-family-safety If you are going this route for Facebook monitoring, you do not need any other monitoring or content filtering tools. This one product will block and filter like K9, as well as monitor and report their activity on Facebook or Twitter like Minor Monitor, all in one package.

* Norton Online Family – If you own Norton Security, Norton 360 or Norton Antivirus, this free add-on offers good control and reporting.

Online Tools To Control Your Network

★ If you do not have a router at your house, sign up and monitor/block traffic with OpenDNS or Norton DNS on the PC. There is no software to install. Just point your computer to their DNS address and sign up (Detailed instructions are in Setting up DNS Resolution). A paid premium version adds some features, but the free version works well.

★ If you have a router in the house, I recommend setting OpenDNS or NortonDNS as the DNS service that the router assigns when computers in the house connect to it. This option will be in your router "LAN" or "wireless" settings (discussed in detail later in the book). These services protect the computers in your home from browsing to known dangerous sites. Both OpenDNS and NortonDNS allow you to point your computer's address resolution service to their list of safe websites. NortonDNS goes one step further: if you choose its pornography blocking DNS settings, it will block pornography sites.

★ NETGEAR Live Parent Controls – free if you own a NETGEAR router, this tool offers additional protection for your house network. www.netgear.com/LPC

★ Other router vendors (Linksys, Belkin, and Trendnet) offer varying degrees of built-in parental control. Read the box or ask someone in the store before you buy.

Specialized Browsers for Kids

★ Peanut Butter PC – A safe kids' browser and a complete kid-safe PC suite of software. www.peanutbuttersoftware.com
★ Kidoz – A safe browser for kids www.kidoz.net

Parental Resources on the Internet

★ www.nap.edu/netsafekids
★ www.wiredsafety.org
★ www.netsmartz.org
★ www.getnetwise.org
★ www.software4parents.com
★ www.cyberangels.org
★ www.wiredsafety.org
★ www.staysafeonline.org
★ www.Safekids.com
★ www.Netsmartz.org
★ www.nap.edu/netsafekids/inter_kids.html

Government Sites for Parental Information

★ www.fbi.gov/stats-services/publications/parent-guide
★ www.fbi.gov/fun-games/kids/kids-safety
★ www.ftc.gov/bcp/menus/consumer/data/child.shtm
★ www.onguardonline.gov
★ www.ftc.gov/youarehere
★ www.nimh.nih.gov/health/publications/suicide-a-major-preventable-mental-health-problem-fact-sheet/suicide-a-major-preventable-mental-health-problem.shtml
★ www.suicidepreventionlifeline.org

House Rules or
'The Family Meeting'

CALL A FAMILY MEETING and design your families do's and don'ts for the Internet. Talk to your family and let them become partners in developing your house rules for using the Internet. Also discuss with your kids and let them suggest consequences for violating these rules. Some rules you can use to start from are included in this *Sample House Internet Rules Contract (Figure 2)*.

Sample House Internet Rules Contract

I, _____, agree to follow the house rules in exchange for Internet privileges.

- Don't share passwords.
- Don't share personal information.
- All pictures must be approved by your parents before emailing, texting, or posting them.
- Use only _____ as your search engine.
- Each person gets _____ hours of computer time a week.
- "Lights out" time for computers, phones, and any portable devices is _____ p.m.
- Do not disable or attempt to defeat the security systems put in place by your parents.
- Never install a program on a computer without getting permission.
- Report any questionable texting, chatting, Facebook messaging, tweet, or email to your parents.
- Your first friend on all "friendable" apps is your parent.
- Be polite.
- _____

Signed: _____ Date: _____

Figure 2: Sample House Internet Rules Contract

Another suggestion was lauded by theatlantic.com as "the most brilliant intersection of parenting and technology since the chore wheel." The advice was pictured on a PostIt™ note that read:

"Want today's Wi-Fi password?

1) Make your beds

2) Vacuum downstairs

3) Walk the dog"

Well played, PostIt™ Mom. Well played.

Do's and Don'ts for Staying Involved

Don't: Young children should not be allowed on the Internet without adult supervision. Explore the Internet WITH your children. Direct them to GOOD sites like PBS, Disney, AOL Kids, and many, many others.

Do: Talk to your children about the Internet.

Do: Teach them good safety rules and behaviors.

Do: Model good behavior for your children.

Do: Talk to your kids about cyberbullying and what to watch for.

Do: Tell your kids that if they see anything odd, different, disturbing, etc., on the web, to talk to you or an adult about it.

Do: Discuss your expectations on computer time with your kids.

Do: Set up a place where you can keep track of what they are doing on the Internet.

Do: Work with them on the Internet. Make Internet time like family TV time – a together activity.

Do: Make use of free and paid-for tools to keep your family safe.

Don't: Teach your children not to "friend" people they or you don't know!

Do: Be your child's first friend on Facebook and first follower on Twitter.

Do: Monitor your child's activity on every device that can communicate with the world. Did you know that some iPod Touch versions can text messages to phones?

Do: Watch activity on Facebook, Google+, YouTube, MySpace, email, text messages, and any other site your children hang out on.

Do: Look in the deleted and trash bins for stuff they tried to hide from you.

Do: Watch how they work on their computers and look for changes in behavior.

Do: Stay connected. Read, learn and try to stay current on what technology is used in your schools and among your kid's friends.

DON'T: DON'T SHARE

Don't Share

STOP SHARING! NO, REALLY! STOP! Your parents were wrong, don't share. Your friends on any social media site don't need to know where you are going, when you are going, how long your house is empty, and so much more information that you give away every day.

Instead of focusing on the "don'ts", let me rephrase this into three "do's":

Do: Pay attention to what you post on line.

Do: Protect your privacy actively.

Do: Only share what you really need to.

Figure 3 is an excellent table of what specifically you and your children should and shouldn't share.

Don't Share	Do Share
• Passwords • Money • Data • Viruses • Tools • Location • Anatomy	• That adorable picture of my guinea pig propped on a generic computer keyboard, providing that the image has no identifying characteristics (or reflections of identifying characteristics) like name plates, diplomas, paperwork, school hoodies, trophies, or anything else that can ultimately tie the photo as belonging to me

Figure 3. What Not to Share.

Sure, it's exciting to share that right now you're standing at the International Peace Gardens with one foot in the United States and one foot in Canada. But, unless you live in Dunseith, North Dakota, you are giving burglars (or teenage ravers) carte blanche on visiting your vacant home. Self-control is your child's best friend when it comes to safeguarding their privacy (and yours) on the Internet. Just like you teach your child to be responsible with her house key, she needs to learn safe habits to keep passwords, money, data, viruses, tools, location and anatomy private. One of the first ways we can keep all of these secure is by instituting and modeling concrete rules about not sharing passwords.

While talking about what not to share, we must mention a great "self-stalking" application called *foresquare*™. *foresquare*™ allows you to "check in" and broadcasts your physical location via social media (i.e., *Kevin Russell is at Happy Happy Burger Fun Time*). I do not recommend letting your child use this application. Checking in with this application on a date is an effective way for your teen to tell everyone, including his last girlfriend, where he is right now and get himself attacked.

Passwords or 'My Baloney Has a First Name...'

"Your password is 'baloney1'? That is a terrible password!"
"Well, it used to be just 'baloney', but now they make you add numbers."
- dialogue from The Hangover Part II

PASSWORDS ARE ONE OF THE MOST FUN TOPICS during my security lectures to people. "Show of hands: how many of you use the name of something near and dear to you as a password?" (Uh, reader, you can put your hand down. This is just an example.) "How many of you are using a word like 'baloney1'?"

What's Your Password?

Anyone ever ask you that question? Did you tell them? I did and became a guinea pig. Lesson learned. My advice for avoiding being transformed into a guinea pig is:

Do: Protect your password.
Do: Keep it to yourself.

Don't: Do not share it.

Do: Change your password *at least* every 6 months.

No tech support or help desk at any institution should ever ask you what your password is. If they do ask for your password, do not give to them. No reputable company will ask for your password.

In many cases the only thing separating you from your comfortable life and spiraling into abject poverty is your password. When was the last time you changed it?

Which password?

All of them! Your banking, your credit card company, your personal email, Facebook, Twitter, Pinterest, Tumblr and, passwords at work. All of them. Using a vulnerable password is like leaving a window open for a cybercriminal.

Now that you are going to change your password, there are some basics you should know about picking a password.

The term "password" is a misnomer. A simple phrase, spaces included if allowed, makes a better password. A simple phrase tends to be longer, easier to type, and more secure. Let's call it a "passphrase".

Choose a strong passphrase. How? Easy: pick something – some phrase or word you will always remember -- and then DON'T use it! Don't use your pet, kid, car, last name, first name, college mascot or anything I could guess based on your Facebook wall. Harsh, right? But the truth is, if you pick something near and dear to you, it is easy to guess. The best passwords are sentences. Many sites will not allow spaces, but you can run the words together. Compare three examples: "N3bra&k@" or "I love the year 2012" or "Ilovetheyear2012". Which is easier to type? Which is easier to remember? You are right. The sentence is easier in both cases, and it is actually a better passphrase.

Next you ask, "What about when I need 5 different passwords?" Easy. Take your favorite fun phrase and add a pattern of letters, numbers or symbols that is unique to each site that requires a password. How do I pick a unique pattern? I look at the "sign-in" screen on each site and pick something from the screen as my pattern. Maybe I take the 5 characters at the topmost right corner and add them to my password phrase. If you are consistent in your passwords, you'll have a reminder on every screen!

Figure 4 is an example of my password strategy using the Walt Disney World ™ website. Our favorite passphrase is "I love 2012 monkeys". On every webpage where I sign in, I take four letters from the upper left corner of the page, exactly as they appear. Looking at the example below, the upper left corner is the word "Disney". Because we always choose the first four letters in the upper left corner, I chose "Disn". The "D" is capitalized because it is capped on the page. After combining my favorite passphrase with the four letters, we get "I love 2012 monkeys Disn". When I sign into to the Disney™ website I will use the passphase "I love 2012 monkeys Disn".

Figure 4: Password example using Disney website

When confronted with those challenge questions that you can use in case you forget your password, what should you choose? Not your real school. Not your real dog's name. Make something up. That way, no matter how much you talk about your dog on Facebook, no one can use that to guess your challenge answer.

Then there are those darn "Security Questions" to reset your password. Use the same common sense here. Your dog's name should not be your reset answer. The same is true for your school, your mom, or the place you met your spouse. What if, regardless of the question, you just used a back-up passphrase like "100 Ants in my pants"? Hmmmm. Note: one flaw in using absurd passphrases is that, should you encounter a problem that requires talking to a genuine human being to reset your password, they will likely ask you the challenge questions. There is a slight possibility that you will sound like a goofball.

Never keep a list of your passwords (or passphrases) on your computer in a text or Word file or anything else that someone could read. If you need to remember many passwords, use a secure password storage tool. They allow you to remember one master password (so make it good!) to access all of your passwords. There are many on the market. KeePass is an example of a free password storage tool.

When you make use of a great tool like KeePass, you become addicted to it. Then you use it for all of your passwords. Then you forget all your passwords because KeePass remembers them for you. Then you leave your laptop in a bar. That is bad in two ways. Your laptop is gone and your passwords, that you no longer remember, are also gone. Here is what I do. I keep my primary KeePass on a USB drive using KeePass' portable version. (This is where my wife began to snicker, "And USB drives don't get lost?") AND! I keep a backup on a desktop computer at my house. If I lose my memory stick, someone can try to crack the double encryption that KeePass uses while I change my passwords to new ones using the backup copy at home. Note to wife: I have never lost my password USB drive.

NEVER SHARE YOUR PASSWORD!!

I don't care if your buddy has a cousin who can level your 55 Tauren Shaman to Level 80 over the weekend for a case of Budweiser. Don't share your password! If you really need your Shaman at Level 80, get a good leveling guide, drink the case of beer, and play the game yourself!

Many Internet protection suites also offer password storage locations. Norton Identity Safe and Norton Access Vault are two examples. Phone-based password vault apps have become very popular. These apps load onto your phone and create an encrypted storage location for your passwords. The theory is that your phone is always with you, so your passwords are also always with you. There are many varieties of apps offering different security options, from password-based to PIN-based to the finger-print based (think: iPhone). My real worry about these is twofold: Is the encryption sound and how often do you lose your phone? Encryption is something you have to take for granted. Either they do it right… or not. I don't use a phone-based password locker. Why not? Well, I don't think I have ever lost my desktop computer. My phone, on the other hand , has been misplaced countless times. Did I lose it while it was unlocked? Hmmm. That could be bad.

Passwords Do's and Don'ts

Do: Choose strong password phrases.

Don't: Avoid anything in your password that someone can find on your Facebook wall.

Don't: Don't use your real pet, school, or mother as your challenge question answer.

Currency or 'Obliterating Your Money Trail'

LET'S LOOK AT WAYS NOT TO SHARE YOUR MONEY (at least not involuntarily). Many people think that using a credit card on the Internet is very dangerous. Actually, using one in person is still more dangerous according to the latest FBI security reports. The other day, my wife got a call from our credit card company. They told her that someone had tried to use our card to purchase something at a major online gaming site. She told them to put the card on hold while we looked into it, because we actually play that game and so do our daughters. I don't always follow my own advice on not installing major time wasters on my computer, but we like the game. We looked into the accounts. We have four different credit cards for four different purposes (you don't have to have four credit cards, but I highly recommend two).

★ The first card is our actual credit card. We use it for shopping and dining, but never on the Internet.

- ★ The second card is for travel because of the travel protection it offers (and the points) but, again, never on the Internet.
- ★ The third card is our Internet shopping card. This is a very low limit card that we use for online shopping, but never in person.
- ★ The fourth card is just for emergencies. Again, like number 1 and 2, this one is not used on the Internet.

I didn't realize that the fraud was not regarding the Internet card until I checked the activity on all four of our gaming accounts. This meant that our card was stolen, not on the Internet, but in person! We called back the credit card company and had them cancel the card. This story backs up the statistics from the FBI.

To Bill Pay or Not to Bill Pay?

A new dilemma has arisen in our already complicated lives. Should we pay our bill by the bank's electronic banking method (web banking) or via the old fashioned mail?
Both.
The best answer is two-fold.

(1) Online banking is a safe and convenient way to pay your bills:
- ★ if you are good about keeping your financial dealings separate from your Facebook computer or the computer that your children use to play games you bought in the bargain bin for $5 (I recommend having two computers);
- ★ if you change your password regularly;
- ★ if you run a good antivirus / firewall program; and
- ★ if you don't browse "those" sites on this computer.

(2) You should think twice about online banking if you don't have two computers at home to separate these two worlds - unless you are very careful in your normal browsing habits and follow all the rules in the

Browsers section of this book. I would definitely use Sandboxie if I wanted to use Social Media and banking on the same machine. Social media has a nasty tendency to open your world to new and exciting ways of compromising your security. Don't even get me started on how cheap kids' games (even those not played on the internet) can trash a computer. We had a terrible time keeping our kids' computers clean and running because every time they installed a CD of a silly bake-a-cake/ride-a-pony/find-a-happy-face game, our system locked up and became virtually useless.

Mailing a bill payment through the mail is not perfectly safe either. If you just drop the outbound payment in the box with the flag up, you are inviting your friendly neighborhood privacy thief to drop by and take said payment out of your mail. You would be horrified by what they can do with a signed check. Check scrubbing is a whole other topic we can talk about another day. I'll bring in my soapbox…

Do's and Don'ts for Paying Bills

Do: If you pay your bills by mail, take them to a post office and put them in the big blue can, not your curbside box, or, YUCK, the communal outbound box at your apartment building!

Do: If you bank online (web banking), get a cheap second computer and use it only for financial work. Reserve this machine for online purchases, banking, tax preparation, check book management, and any other thing that involves your private data. I know this sounds extravagant or paranoid, but it is not. Social networking sites, games sites, and "those" sites are riddled with viruses, and you do not want to mix them with your financial work. Since you are about to upgrade your computer anyway, don't get rid of the old system. Reload it with a new operating system, update its antivirus and firewall (more on this in _Configuration of Your Computer_), and use it only to shop, bank, and manage your financial life. Now, on your Internet machine, you may social network, browse "those" sites, and play online games. Just be prepared to wipe and rebuild this system regularly!

Do: Run and keep your antivirus software current. Make sure your antivirus program is set to automatically update (instructions in *Antivirus / Antispyware*).

Do: Keep the system up-to-date with patches by Microsoft (detailed instructions in *Set Auto Update to On*).

Do: Make sure your Internet security package firewall is on and running (detailed instructions in *Computer Firewall*).

Do: Install additional protection tools like "Threatfire" or "Immunet" (see *Configuration of Your Computer*).

Shop 'til You Lock

Shopping on the Internet at stores that are legitimate is actually safer that handing your credit card to someone you don't know who takes it out of your sight. I am not saying that the Internet is safe; but, if you are careful, you may find it is safer than the physical world.

Look for the lock. Every browser has a way to show you that the website where you are shopping is protecting the information that you are typing. Many display a little padlock somewhere on the screen. Others change the color of the address bar. Google Chrome™ presents a lock to the left of the address bar and the HTTPS is in green. Microsoft Internet Explorer shows a lock at the right side of the address bar or on the bottom right of the screen in the status bar (see the example in *Figure 5*).

Figure 5: Microsoft IE on HTTPS

In Mozilla Firefox™, look for the lock or verify that the address starts with HTTPS (See the example in *Figure 6* of Firefox with https displayed). No matter what browser you use, the "S" should be at the end of HTTP every time you are about to enter personal information. Think HTTPS: "S" for "secure".

Figure 6: Firefox on HTTPS

Do's and Don'ts for Safe Shopping

Do: Look for the lock.

Do: Know who they are… Shop at stores you trust. Only give your credit card info to the names you trust, like Disney, Target, Amazon, Best Buy, Wal-Mart, Sears, or other reputable names that you recognize. If you don't know the store, check with the Better Business Bureau (www.bbb.org). They rate the validity and safety of most online merchants. If a site is not listed with the BBB, consider shopping elsewhere.

Don't: Don't fall for fake bargains. If the deal is too good to be true, IT IS!

Do: Get a separate credit card for Internet shopping and confirm its Internet protection policy. Make sure your Internet card has a charging limit that is low. My wife and I were sadly surprised when our Internet credit card company rewarded us for being good customers by raising our credit limit.

Don't: Do not carry your Internet card in your wallet.

Don't: NEVER USE YOUR DEBIT CARD! Why not? There are different protection levels offered on normal credit cards versus debit cards. Your debit card is linked directly to your bank account and thieves could potentially clean out your entire account. Check with your bank on their policies for debit cards. Many banks offer the same protection as a credit card, but not all do.

Do: Review credit card bills carefully each month. Are there excessive charges? Duplications? Unknown merchants?

Do: Remember that credit card information is stolen from retail sites on the Internet every day.

Do: Use a service like PayPal™ to keep your credit card/bank account info away from vendors. PayPal offers a "Security Key" that you can use to protect your account with almost unbreakable security. You can even use your mobile phone as the key! You can use PayPal™ at many major retailers (*Figure 7*).

🛒 Your Info   Delivery Info   **Payment**   Review & Submit   Order Complete

PAYMENT INFORMATION

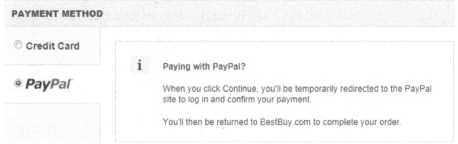

Figure 7: Best Buy accepting PayPal

Don't: Do not shop at stores or enter your credit card information if the browser does not show a secure connection... Remember "The Lock".

Data or

'Secret Agent Man'

WE ALL GENERATE AND STORE INFORMATION. Some public information that you have probably shared this month includes:

★ Name
★ Address
★ Property
★ Phone number
★ Anything you've posted on a social media site.

Examples of private information that you want to protect from sharing are:

★ Social Security Number
★ Credit card numbers
★ Financial records (often stored on your computer) like tax returns, checkbook, and stock portfolios
★ Passwords
★ Pictures.

What Data Is On Your Computer?

Why should you care where your data is or what is on your computer? If you are like more than 90% of the computer owners in America, you connect your computer to the Internet. In the every-changing environment of the Internet, even the most careful of us are at risk of having predators invade our data. Let's make them work for it, shall we?

Take a mental inventory of everything on your computer. Check the sources, email, social media accounts, checkbook management, tax preparation software, etc.

Identify where the data is and remove it or block access to it. I move all of my private data to an encrypted folder. Encryption tools make a folder on your computer unreadable to anyone without the password. Free encryption products like VeraCrypt or inexpensive products like SecureZip allow you to encrypt and lock folders with a password. These tools make it easy to keep data on your computer private.

What Data Is In Your Cloud?

It is hard to escape "the cloud" today. Everywhere you look, you will see it mentioned. If you purchase a tablet, it likely came preloaded with a cloud interface like Dropbox or box or Evernote. All Windows 8 computers come with a connection to the Microsoft OneDrive. Your phone even wants to backup your music and movies to the cloud.

Cloud backup services can be great places to put your data to protect you from a computer crash or hard drive failure. Typical cloud services are Microsoft OneDrive, Google Drive, Dropbox, Evernote, and iCloud. All these cloud storage services store your information in the cloud. Where is the cloud, you ask? It is wherever your provider put it – not on your computer, tablet, iPad, or phone, but on their computers in their data centers around the world. Is your data safe in the cloud? In most cases, it is safe… to an extent. While most reputable services from big name players treat your data with respect, you still must be careful about what you put in the cloud. I would avoid storing documents with Social Security numbers or tax returns unless the service is specifically encrypted for sensitive data. Also, less scrupulous providers may bury clauses in their user agreements giving them rights to your data. Read the EULA (End User License Agreement) to determine who owns the data, you or them?

Backing up your phone to the cloud via your phone carrier or Apple's iCloud can be a great way to protect your data. Keep in mind that you are also giving them a copy of your contacts, your apps, the data your apps have collected, and your pictures.

The cloud also makes it easy to move data from one computer to another or access your files from your mom's house. As my wife likes to point out to me, it is far more likely that her computer will crash and burn, taking her unpublished novel with it, than a sleazy contractor from her cloud service stealing the document and publishing it as his own. Personally, I stand by my dyed-in-the-wool security viewpoint: if you are writing the great American novel, you might want to keep it local so no one else can claim copyright over it. An example: This book you are reading was stored on my cloud backup, but only after it was copyrighted and published. Then I felt safe putting a copy on the cloud, when my computer started to act up.

My Shredder, My Friend

I come home from work every day only to find another batch of credit card offers, blank checks from my credit card companies, and every other manor of solicitation with my name, address, phone number (even how much I owe on my mortgage!), already filled out for my convenience. What a nightmare. All that a good privacy thief needs to take over my financial life is bundled in a Hefty™ bag and set on my front berm each week.

What should you do with all this trash?

Meet "Shredder", your new best friend. … What?!? … You don't have a shredder?

STOP right here, go out and get one. They are cheap and an essential part of your basic supplies for life. Make sure you get a "cross cut" or "confetti" shredder. They even come in pink.

No, go now, I will wait.......... Continue reading when you are back with the new shredder.

Now that you have your shredder, keep it plugged in near where you deal with the mail.

What goes into the shredder? Everything with your name and address on it. Shred away.

To add to your shredding fun, on the day that you dump your shredding add a little security technique that I like to call "creative waste management". The days as a pet owner (note: you can also replace "pet owner" with "new parent") that you have to do the "clean up" part of pet maintenance are the best days to throw away your shredded material or anything else that may have private information on it. As you get the daily batch of credit card offers, shred them and put the shreds with the used diapers or with the cat litter. Creative waste management: putting your private materials into trash that only the truly desperate would dig through and, thus, increasing your level of security. What could keep a would-be privacy thief out of your old credit card information more than cat urine! I take things a step further, by never tossing all bits of a shredded credit card in the same bag. So mix and match your trash, use "creative waste management", and protect your identity!

The Shred List

What to shred? Only shred if you are going to throw it away.

- ☐ Shred anything in the mail with your name on it
- ☐ Address labels from junk mail and magazines
- ☐ ATM receipts
- ☐ Bank statements
- ☐ Birth certificate copies
- ☐ Canceled and voided checks

- [ ] Checks from your credit card company
- [ ] Credit and charge card bills, carbon copies, summaries and receipts
- [ ] Credit reports and histories
- [ ] Documents containing maiden name (used by credit card companies for security reasons)
- [ ] Documents containing names, addresses, phone numbers or email addresses
- [ ] Documents relating to investments
- [ ] Documents containing passwords or PIN numbers
- [ ] Driver's licenses or items with a driver's license number
- [ ] Employee pay stubs
- [ ] Employment records
- [ ] Expired passports and visas
- [ ] Un-laminated identification cards (college IDs, state IDs, employee ID badges, military IDs)
- [ ] Legal documents
- [ ] Investment, stock and property transactions
- [ ] Items with a signature (leases, contracts, letters)
- [ ] Luggage tags
- [ ] Medical and dental records
- [ ] Papers with a Social Security number
- [ ] Pre-approved credit card applications
- [ ] Receipts with checking account numbers
- [ ] Report cards
- [ ] Resumes or curriculum vitae
- [ ] Tax forms
- [ ] Transcripts
- [ ] Travel itineraries
- [ ] Used airline tickets
- [ ] Utility bills (telephone, gas, electric, water, cable TV, Internet)

Data Privacy Do's and Don'ts

Do: Shred everything you don't keep. If it has your name on it shred it.

Don't: Do not share everything about you. Stop.

Do: Encrypt things on your computer.

Do: Stick to reputable names for your cloud storage and read the license to make sure you know their rules.

Viruses or 'Inoculating against the File-Sharing Flu'

WHERE DO VIRUSES COME FROM? This is a much easier topic than 'where do babies come from?', though equally complicated, confusing, and flustering.

Not exactly. Viruses come from infected files. Infected files get to your computer from infected websites, email downloads, and file downloads. The most common viruses carrier is…you. Yes, you. You opened an email of questionable nature and then downloaded the attachment. When your antivirus software asked you if it should allow some activity, you said "YES". Why did you say "YES?" Be careful where you browse and do not click in a pop-up unless you know why it is there. Do not download files from free sharing services. It's stealing and many of the files are infected.

When your antivirus program detects that a program is being installed onto your system, regardless of whether the program is good, bad, or indifferent, the antivirus program will generate a pop-up asking you if you want to install the program. If you are installing a common, benign file, the pop-up may include a recommendation to continue. If it does not recognize the program and suspects a virus, the pop-up will warn you with a bright red message. If you were not actively trying to install something you know to be clean, now would be a good time to stop the process. If you were just reading your email, you should ask, "If I am just reading email, why is something installing?" – another good time to hit the NO button.

You will hear the term "malware" throughout this book. What do I mean by "malware"? Malware is the general term for malicious software, programs, scripts, and other executable code that does something bad.

* Computer viruses are a form of malware that install or run a program on your computer that will damage files or worse.
* Spyware is a form of malware that installs a program on your computer that will gather information about you (user ids and passwords, credit card numbers, or Social Security numbers) and pass that information on to the bad guys.
* Browser cookies can be malware if they are trying to gather information about you that you do not want to share.
* Email spam often contains malware or links that will try to install viruses or spyware on your computer.
* Antivirus programs like Norton, McAfee, Comodo, AVG, and most of the others are really anti-malware programs, not just antivirus.

"Hackers" is a term used for any person or group that is creating software to do something on your computer without your knowledge. The term hacker has changed significantly over time. A hacker in the 70s and 80s was a person who "hacked" at computer hardware and software to build a better system. Many of the most famous computer leaders of today were originally called "hackers", back when it was positive term or compliment. Today, though, the term hacker has been popularized by the media as only negative. Now a "hacker" is someone who is trying to do things that are often illegal or immoral.

"Script Kiddies" are usually young people who have just started "hacking" and are using tools written by more advanced "hackers" instead of inventing their own tools. Serious hackers are still not very common. The level of skill and knowledge it takes to achieve the elite designation of "hacker" is substantial, and very few people in the world have that skill. Script Kiddies are far more common because the level of skill and knowledge is less. Some Script Kiddies will continue to practice their art and become true hackers.

Security risks aren't just limited to particular software. Hackers exploit flaws found in any software, even quality software from Microsoft, Mozilla, Apple, Adobe, Google, and many others that we rely on every day. Most firms rapidly fix the flaws or release new versions. In *Configuration of Your Computer*, you will learn how to adjust your *System and Security* settings to notify you of Microsoft updates. Please update all your software weekly.

Interesting statistics from the researchers at McAfee:

★ 40% of password stealers are associated with gaming and virtual worlds (social media).
★ 80% of banking emails are phishing scams.

Figure 8 below shows a fantastic example of how to recognize a fraudulent (phishing) email. The folks at Wells Fargo Bank should be commended for providing this excellent example on their web site at https://www.wellsfargo.com/privacy_security/fraud/operate/emails. They also provide some fantastic suggestions for red flags that can help alert you to suspect fraudulent phishing. My wife's favorite is poor spelling or grammar that suggests the authors used a bad translation program to convert the email from their language to English.

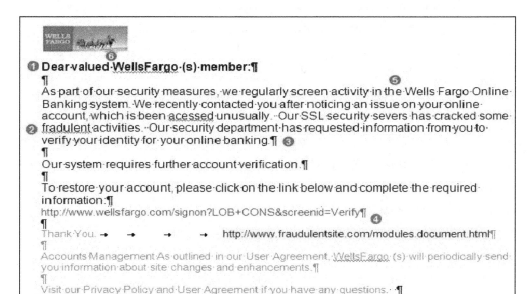

1. **Awkward greeting**
A phish may address the customer with a nonsensical greeting or may not refer to the customer by name.

2. **Typos**
This isn't because fraudsters don't know how to spell – it's so the phish won't be blocked by email filters.

Examples in this phish: "acessed" "Our SSL security severs has…" "fradulent"

3. **Incorrect grammar**
Another tactic used to bypass email filters.

Examples in this phish: "Our SSL security severs has…"

4. **Strange or unfamiliar links**
This link looks official, but notice what happens when the mouse curser rolls over it. The link's source code points to a completely different web site. Remember that you can always type a URL into your web browser instead of clicking on a link.

5. **Compelling or urgent language**
An urgent need to communicate with you for your own security, or a request to update your information immediately.

Examples in this phish: "We recently contacted you after noticing an issue on your online account, which has been acessed unusually."
"Our security department has requested information from you to verify your identity for your online banking."

6. **Mis-spelled company name.**
Another tactic used to bypass email filters.

Example in the phish: "WellsFargo (s)"

Figure 8: Wells Fargo example of Phishing. Pulled from
https://www.wellsfargo.com/privacy_security/fraud/operate/emails on 08/25/2012

Music, Movies, TV, Videos, Books, and Term Papers or 'Oh My!'

MANY PEOPLE LIKE TO PURCHASE music, movies, television, videos, and books on the Internet. If you do this, follow safe Internet shopping techniques, and you should be fine. However, if you decide to go to one of the many "file sharing" sites and get your music, books, or videos for free, there are a few things you should think about.

★ Unless your child has downloaded directly from a site owned by a record company, or TV studio, or band that is giving away one song to get you interested, she is likely, albeit unknowingly, stealing. A file-sharing site that allows downloads of copyrighted works is illegal. The person who created that material would most likely want to be paid for his or her work. By grabbing it for free, your son or daughter is doing the same thing as going into the drugstore, sticking that pack of gum in a pocket, and walking out without paying: stealing.

★ You have a much higher probability of infecting your computer with a virus or other malware. The top box office movie that you can download for "free" is a great Trojan horse for sneaking a virus onto your computer. In fact, many hackers "justify" giving you a virus, saying that it's just karmic justice to break the computer of someone who was stealing in the first place. This is true for any "get something for nothing" scam. They don't care that your child has simply stumbled onto what he saw as a great opportunity to stretch this week's allowance.

A security professional that I know did a test recently. He purchased the same song at Amazon and at Apple. Then he downloaded the same song from a popular "file sharing" site (don't try this at home; it was technically not legal, although the argument can be made that he paid for the same song twice before downloading it for free). He reviewed the three files. The files from Amazon and Apple were the same size, while the file from the download site was 35% larger. Why would this be? The songs were the same length, format, file type, compression ratio, and sampling rate, so why would one be larger? The answer was disturbing. The extra 35% was what we in the security industry call "payload". It was malware designed to record keystrokes and send them to someone. By downloading the song illegally, he had infected his test computer with malware that would steal his bank passwords, credit card numbers, and any other user ids or passwords that he typed.

How would you know that file was filled with bad stuff before you downloaded it? There is no real way to do this, but there are good safety precautions you can use to keep from getting bad files. Think twice before you download files, and teach your children to avoid these sites altogether.

The most common file sharing sites that share infected files are the pornographic sites that are free.

YouTube is a very popular video site that is legal. The team at YouTube strives to keep your family safe by diligently scrubbing (or searching) their files every day to identify and remove files that are illegal or carrying payload. But hackers keep posting infected files, hoping that you will download them before YouTube catches them. Many companies, news agencies, and schools use this site to share video clips. While there are many valid and safe uses of YouTube, you need to instruct your children to be careful on YouTube. Random posts on YouTube by people or companies you don't know can contain malware. If you simply cannot resist following the continuing adventure of Charlie the Unicorn on YouTube, do not do so on your banking computer.

At our house we purchase music and movies through three popular outlets. All three accounts are in either my wife's or my name. Did you know that you can connect your entire family's collection of music players (mp3, iPod, phone) to one Apple iTunes account? I allow my children to purchase whatever music they want with their money, but through my account. That way, I know what they are spending and what they own. The same is true for movies and books. This way I will know if a movie we didn't purchase shows up on my kid's computer.

A thought on plagiarism: the Internet is full of great resources. Using it to do research for school papers is just about required by our schools from 6th grade until college. I cannot image how my wife and I survived school before the Internet. Oh, wait, we used that set of 1974 World Book Encyclopedias from the school library. Today though, our children can cheat by using the Internet to search for just about any topic, specify the grade level of the report needed, and download a complete report. All they do is put their name on it and turn it in. Most school systems have figured this out, and many teachers actually do sentence searches on the Internet on papers that they think are above the level of the student who called it her own. Even copying sections of web pages directly from the page to their report is tricky if they do not site their source properly. This is a form of plagiarism that can lead to your child being kicked out of school, which leaves more time for them to collect apps on their computer.

Apps or *'Should You Have Them All?'*

ARE YOU AN APP JUNKIE? Does your system seem slower and slower and slower all the time? Maybe you have too many applications. Delete or clean up apps that you are not using.

So you have just discovered a blog stream that talks about the coolest app you can ever imagine. Just load it up right? Well, hold on just one moment. Let's ask a couple of basic questions.

* Is this your work machine?
* Does your company have software license and installation rules (like mine does)?
* Is the app too good to be free? If so, it likely came with some un-intended payload like a Trojan or virus or worm. Some are free for real, offered by companies to get your interest in their paid-for products. A good example of this is the antivirus industry. Many vendors (McAfee, Norton, Trend Micro, Kasperky, and Comodo) offer free "light" versions or timed version of their product to get

you to buy the "full" version. They have a vested interest in your satisfaction.

★ Did you search for reviews of your app by major magazines (PC World, CNET, etc.)? If the product has been reviewed, it is probably real. On the flipside, before you load an app you can search the Internet for the app's name and then 'security concerns'. You might find an article that could save your personal bacon.

★ Did you check the install file for viruses before you started the install? That will work 40% of the time. Otherwise, your file verification software (i.e., Immunet or ThreatFire; see Reputation Based File Verification) is your best protection.

★ Did your firewall send you any red alerts? Did you read the message in the pop-up? I have experienced instances where the only way I avoided a virus was through my antivirus alert system, warning me about traffic to the Internet. Notice that I said "to the Internet". When you download an app, you should be receiving traffic from the Internet, not transmitting your data to the Internet.

Remember, think before you load.

Email or
"What Not To Open"

"HE SENT A PICTURE OF WHAT?" I heard a human resources director say incredulously one day on the phone. When she got the call, I just happened to be in her office talking about another employee sending email that really should not have been sent.

I find email funny. Why? People treat email like some private, secure form of communication. At work. Hmmm. If I came to your house and started using your toaster, would that make it my toaster?

"That's ridiculous," you are now thinking.

"Not so," I say.

Email is a shared medium. What do I mean by that? Email has to be transmitted from your computer to the person you sent it to. That transmission system is very much like the phone system of the early 1900's, when a person had to physically connect your call by plugging in a wire. Today computers make this connection, but your email will still stop several places along the way (*Figure 9*).

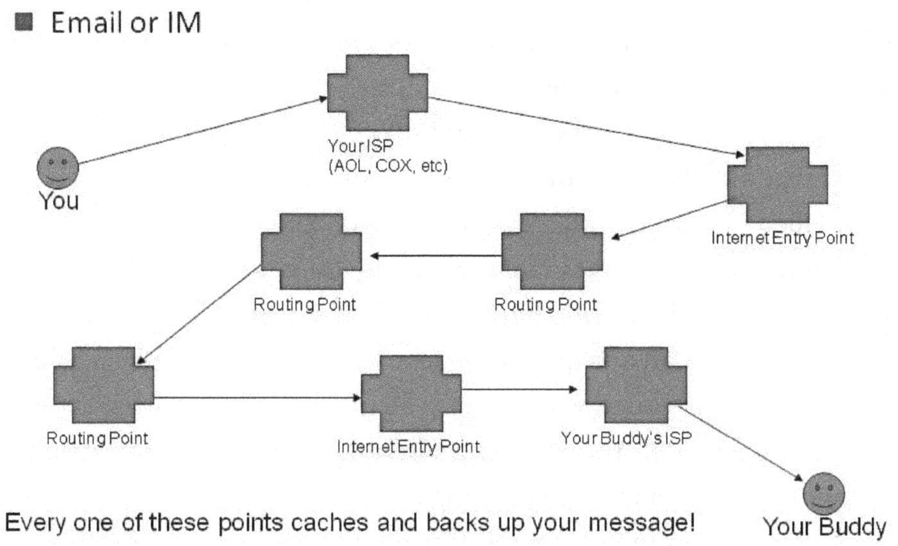

Email or IM

Figure 9: Email Routing

Should these stops worry you? Normally, no. These stops just pass your email along to its destination. If you are doing something illegal or something you want to keep secret, then, yes these stops should concern you. You should know that at many of these stops your email is stored and backed up. This means that they have a copy of your email forever! My advice in email is to only send something you are comfortable having the whole world see.

People treat their work email like it is theirs. They treat their work computer like it is theirs. But neither is true. The company that you work for owns both. While many employees can expect some sort of privacy at work, know that your company can and will monitor your activity, be it instant messaging, website access or email. Even if you carefully delete your browser history, email history, and trash can, your company has a copy of these items in their back-ups. We will discuss how you can use tools to monitor your child's behavior on the internet in *Configuration of Your Computer*. These tools are mini-versions of the ones that your company has installed to watch YOU. If anything that you are doing on this equipment can even remotely be construed as illegal, immoral, or fattening, know that, when push comes to shove, the company will hand over your email to the authorities in a heartbeat. The moral of the story is: don't send stuff at work (be it in email, instant message, Skype, or Jabber…) that you do not want someone else to read, share, printout, send to other people, or ridicule. Now would be a great time to ask your buddies to remove you from their hate mail / porn / illegal gambling blasts, so you do not receive them at work.

Email is the most common vector for identity theft attackers. More computers are infected by email attachments than any other attack method. Never download an email attachment, unless you are sure that it is real and you need it. Also, never open your email system, unless your virus software is running in active mode. You can use the settings in your email system to protect yourself from accidentally opening a bad email. *Figure 10* shows the Mail Settings for AOL. I recommend setting "Hide images & disable links in mail from unknown senders" and "Notify me before opening mail containing pictures". With these enabled, if your email contains a picture or unknown link, you will have to select "Show images and enable links" prior to viewing it. If you don't know who sent you the email or why you received it or it just doesn't make sense, don't click on "enable". This can protect you from taking a wild ride to virus town.

Figure 10: Mail Settings on AOL.

Junk or Dangerous Mail: How Do You Know Not To Open It?

How can you tell if the email you are about to open is real or fake? How can you tell whether it will infect your computer or not?

Much spam is obvious. The email is from someplace you have never heard of and the subject offers you a product or service that you don't want or need. But not all bad email is spam.

Many of today's identity scams or thefts start with an email message that sounds real. The most common approach is to send you an email that is from someone you know or a company you do business with (see also *Wells Fargo Bank phishing example*). How do you tell if the email is bad?

Don't: If the subject of the email sounds odd, question it, and don't open it.

Don't: If the email is from YOURSELF, don't open it. This is a common and effective way for attackers to get you to open their mail.

Don't: If you get an email from a friend with a subject of "Free car" or "Pictures of …." something you don't want to see or they would never send you, don't open it.

Don't: Do not download an attachment to an email unless you are certain it is real. Attachments to email are the number one way viruses and identity theft programs are installed on computers!

Don't: If the email you've just opened contains a link… don't click on it unless you a SURE it goes where you think. Most banks and credit card companies will not send you email with a link to follow to gather information from you. The identity thieves will.

Don't: Email is not a good place to send images and videos of questionable nature. It can be intercepted many places along the way. Many companies have policies about such imagery, and you may get the recipient in trouble.

Do: If you accidentally open a suspect email or click on a strange link, watch for pop-ups from your antivirus software. If none appear, close all active programs on your computer and run a full system scan, using your antivirus and your reputation-based file verification tool.

The Most Common Email Scam

I hear about this one every month. There is an email type that is circling the Internet and it is mostly targeting older people. The email claims to be from a family member in trouble that needs money. There are many reasons for their supposed distress, but they all involve you sending money to a foreign address. These emails usually contain a real family member's name and some relevant fact (see *Social Media* for a discussion on where they found this information). The information is convincing enough that many older people have sent the money. A confirming phone call can usually set everyone's mind at ease. Please talk to your family about this scam.

Spam

Spam, or the annoying, unsolicited email advertisements that we all get, plague us at a level that junk mail could never attain. There are a few simple do's and don'ts for dealing with spam:

Don't: NEVER RESPOND to spam. Doing so will only let the spammer know that the email address they spammed is valid and attached to a live person. Responding will increase your volume of spam email, because they will sell your email address as a confirmed recipient for even more money.

Don't: NEVER UNSUBSCRIBE. Doing so will only let the spammer know that the email address they spammed is valid and attached to a live person. Sound familiar? Trying to unsubscribe will increase your volume of spam email.

Do: Forward it to your Internet service provider's spam control group. This can be done on AOL by forwarding it to "TOSPAM" or clicking on "Report Spam". Your Internet service provider will have spam blocking tools that you can (and should) use.

Don't: Never download an attachment that you weren't expecting. As I said earlier, attachments are the most common carriers of malware.

Don't: Please don't forward those chain mail messages. Those just add to the already ridiculous volume of email junk that we all have to filter out every day.

Scams or 'Fool Me Once...'

SCAMS ARE ALL TOO COMMON on the Internet. Even legitimate websites that you visit can become infected. Normally safe websites might be running infected ads. This is usually not the fault of the website owner; they may not know they are infected.

Browser scams usually open a pop-up window on your computer that offers you something or asks you a question. Often they look like the website you were on, and they are asking for more information about you. One of the most common browser scams opens a window on your screen and tells you that your system is infected with a virus. The screen has a button on it to "fix" the problem. <u>Do Not Push</u> this button. It will infect you with a real virus. Simply close the pop-up window.

The best way to close a pop-up window is <u>not</u> by clicking on the "X" in the upper right corner. Some particularly clever scams hide links or commands that will damage your computer under a fake "X" in the corner of the pop-up. Instead, head to the bottom of the screen, right click on your browser's icon on the start bar (*Figure 11*).

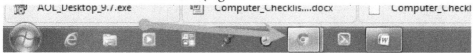

Figure 11: Google Chrome™ browser icon on the start bar

Click "Close all windows" (*Figure 12*). This will close your browser along with the popup. If you only want to close the popup (not quite as safe), see *Antivirus / Anti-spyware*.

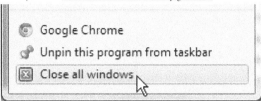

Figure 12. Closing the browser window

If you are running Windows 8.1, you must go to the desktop to see the icon bar shown in *Figure 11*. But you can still right click and close the browser as shown in *Figure 12*.

A very common scam arrives via email. We all see "spam" mail: mail that advertises stuff we really don't want or need. The more dangerous and insidious kind sends mail that looks like it came from your bank, credit card company, the IRS, you name it. These want you to follow a link inside them, to provide them with information, or to visit a site to "fix" your personal information. These emails look legitimate and usually inform you that "Due to a security breach we need to validate your information…. Follow this link: _____". This link takes you to a site that LOOKS like the correct site. You enter your information … and they use it against you (see also *Wells Fargo Bank phishing example*).

What do you do if you suspect a scam? Most of the time, just deleting these emails is enough. If one was particularly disturbing to you, contact impersonated company and ask how to forward the fake message to them so that they can inform other customers.

Never follow a link in an email unless you are absolutely certain that the link is real. If you are at all worried, then open a NEW browser and go to the company, bank, or institution by typing in their address like you normally would. Do not type the web address that the spammers have so helpfully supplied you in their suspicious email.

Social Media or
"Who Needs Frenemies?"

WOW, THE STUFF PEOPLE SHARE in their social media accounts! Should my child post a picture of what she chose to wear today and every day? What about telling everyone on the planet that she is going to see the next great movie at 9 pm at the Happy Theater Chain? And do all of her friends really need to know that she drank twelve 15-ounce glasses of tea today? Can you say "self-stalker?" Armed only with those three posts, a negatively-motivated person can pick her out by her sneakers in the bathroom stall of the theater at 10 p.m. Odds are that such a stalker has not gone to this trouble to deliver a birthday card.

Worse are the people who load their account with every conceivable bit of information about themselves. Now I know their name, address, phone number, school, old school, graduation date, name of your first, last, and latest failed relationship.... By publishing all of this information for the world to see, they are creating their own future identity theft.

Social media has become such a part of our society that people think it's unusual if you do not have a Facebook page. Unfortunately, most people only see the positive part of social media and not the dangerous part. Everything that you post on Facebook, Google+, MySpace, Twitter, etc., is being gathered and used by the businesses that sponsor those companies. If you think only conspiracy nuts believe that these social media giants are selling your information to anyone they can, then ask yourself, "How did Facebook become a billion dollar company if their product is free?" Your information is mined to sell to companies so they can make better marketing decisions. With every friend you add to your Facebook, Google+, Twitter, etc., you are adding another layer of people who have access to everything you write and post.

Social media can be fun and useful, but it needs to come with some basic rules.

The same rules that apply to real life should apply to your child's social media account activity. You taught your children not to talk to strangers. Don't allow them to talk to strangers online. Children seem to think it's acceptable to approve friend requests from perfect strangers, when they would run away from that person on the street. There is no difference. A stranger in social media is actually more dangerous than in real life. Once friended, they can access your child's information at any time day or night. They can gather information about her for years, with her permission, before using it against her.

Before you set up your child's social media account, read their rules. Facebook and Twitter both require a minimum age of 13. It terrifies me to think of all the dangers an 8-year-old faces on Facebook, a place designed for adults to share with other adults. When you set up your children's social media accounts, be very stingy with the information you put into their profile. Don't use your address and phone number. Never put in their school information.

I was at church one Sunday teaching a class on social media safety when one of the women in my class said, "Yesterday I got a friend request from a gentleman who went to my high school. This was strange, since Stanley died 25 years ago."

I love that story. But it is common. If my student had not realized Stanley was deceased and had accepted the friend request, she would have allowed someone with nefarious intent into her friend circle, where they would have had access to anything that she and her friends posted, be it photos of grandchildren or seemingly innocuous references to being on vacation. This is an example of one of the growing number of scams against older people, so you may want to share this advice with <u>your</u> own parents.

Your Passwords and Social Media

A very smart doctoral student at a college in the US used his fellow doctoral candidates to conduct an informal test with surprising results. He asked their permission to attempt to hack into their bank account and move $1. He promised to let them know the minute that he had compromised their accounts, so that they could reset their passwords and see that the dollar really was moved. With four weeks of work he managed to break into every one of their checking accounts and move that dollar. Where did he get the information he needed to break in? From their social media accounts. From their walls, photos and posts, he was able to collect clues on their pets' names, maiden names, birth places, children's names, dates of anniversaries, and anything else they loved. From here, it was simple trial and error to crack their passwords. People tend to talk about the things most important to them – the very things that they think about when asked to invent a password or provide information about the password reset challenge questions. Please remember this story when you choose your passwords.

Set strong passwords on you social media accounts and do not use the same password over and over. Pick a new password for every account. See my section on _Passwords_ to see how I make this a little easier for myself.

Do's and Don'ts for Social Media

Don't: NEVER post where you are GOING!!! Just don't do it. If you are going on vacation, why tell the world that your house is empty for the next two weeks?

Do: Only post where you have been. Talk about how much fun the vacation <u>was</u>, now that you are home.

Don't: NEVER, EVER, post where you are GOING!!! If your child is going on a date, do not let them post where they will be going so an ex-girlfriend can show up and ruin it. Or worse, kick someone's butt!

Don't: Avoid talking about the date at all. It will only make someone mad!

Don't: Never say mean things. Just like at home, Mom is right. If you can't say something nice, don't say anything at all. Keeping your fingers still (or your figurative mouth shut) can save you from getting your butt kicked or worse!

Do: Assume that everyone online is lying! Many 13-year-old girls on social media are neither girls nor thirteen. Some could be creepy old men! The flipside is also true. Your seventeen-year-old son needs to know that many 19-year-old girls on social media are twelve-year-old girls lying about their age to qualify for the account. Among our children's friends, the most popular age these little girls pick is 19.

Don't: Never use your full name, your age, your hometown, your school, your......etc. This is where you create a "persona". Be one of the liars.

Do: Using your name is okay, if you do not use city, school, other traceable information. Keep the info to a minimum. You do not need to complete every profile question (or even most of them). Answer only those that are essential.

Don't: Your child should know that they should never meet someone from the Internet in person. NEVER! (Come to think of it, this is probably a good rule of thumb for the adults in your house, too).

Do: If you must post pictures of yourself, be aware of where it was taken. Are you in your bedroom? What is behind you in the picture? Are there awards with your name and school. Is the mirror showing more of you than you intended or other telltale artifacts? Can a stalker zoom in to read your house number?

And the big one: What are you wearing? (This has nothing to do with nudity.)

This is one of my favorite topics when I speak to youth groups and student gatherings. How many of you have pictures on your social media (personal website, Google+ , Facebook, etc.)? What are you wearing in those pictures? No, I am not talking about sexy clothing. That is not why I am asking (although, if that is where your mind went, then you really should examine what you are wearing in those pictures).

Two examples are a high school girl and a co-worker of mine; two very different people, with the same story. Both were fairly careful about what they posted, to try to keep some part of their lives private. But then they put pictures up on their social media accounts. Both were fully clothed (in fact, both were wearing coats). The high school girl was wearing a letter jacket. Oops, now I know her high school, sport, and name. The co-worker posed in front of her home office "wall of fame", which included her diplomas from both high school and college and some other awards. Yep, now I know her full name, the schools she attended, her major (and GPA based on one of the awards), and some of her volunteerism interests.

Why make it easier for the stalkers to learn stuff about you that you or your child did not intend to publish? Remember, the more that you post about you or your child, the more that bad people know about you and can use against you. If your child lists all of his hobbies, activities, favorite bands, or friends, the bad people have a much easier time making themselves sound interesting to him.

Remember to balance the cool with the safe!

Facebook or 'The Quiz about Me Show'

"How much do my friends know about me?" is a question often asked in the Facebook community. How do you find out? Build a quiz, of course!! Before your child does, maybe the question you should ask first is, "How much should friends know about her?" A recent quiz crossed my spouse's virtual desk from a good friend of hers. It asked, "simply to fill out a quiz about ..." I have to admit, I am security person and more cautious that most, so a quiz that asks how much I know about someone seems both a little sycophantic and a lot intrusive. So we looked at the quiz. After the 5th question, I could have applied for a loan under her friend's name and gotten it, or made a phone transfer of funds from her bank. Sharing all of this is bad enough among "friends", but what if it were blasted across the Internet? There is a scam quiz-builder out there that "helps" you build quizzes for your friends while actually doing two things: first, it builds the quiz, but then it pharms you (Yep, I spelled that right. "Pharming" is wanna-be hacker slang for farming information about you without you knowing they did it) for personal information that it sends to various websites around the world.

Getting to know your friends is great and important - we are social animals - but keeping a certain level of privacy along the way is also important.

By now, you may have concluded that my advice to parents is to teach their children not to share. This might lead some to adjust their information so it is even harder to track them down in real life. This is a good idea. Be careful though, do not impersonate or suggest to your child that they impersonate another real person. Leaving information out is good, falsifying information is dangerous. Pretending to be your best friend can only get you in trouble (maybe even arrested).

Hey! Your child loves filling out those Top Five lists in Facebook? Who doesn't?

Think only your child's friends are reading those? Most people believe that usually only friends of friends are reading those. But are there more? Of course. Nothing is free. So who is paying for those Top Five lists? The company that creates those lists for Facebook sells the results to marketing companies. Does that bother you? It may or may not, depending on your view on privacy. Did you know that your child gave them permission to sell her opinions? When she signed onto Facebook, she signed the End User License Agreement (EULA) and probably didn't even read it. By signing that, she gave them permission to use her Facebook data for research, marketing, and other uses. Every time she pushes the little blue button "ALLOW" on any game or application or quiz, she allows that game's publisher access to her profile information and the contents of what she did in that game, quiz, or application.

People seem to think that much of what they do on the Internet is private.

- ★ Where they browse → Tracked
- ★ Where they shop → Tracked
- ★ Their family photos on Facebook or MySpace → viewable by friends of friends or more

Basically, everything that you or your children do on the Internet leaves your house and your control, as it travels around the globe on wires, stopping along the way to be recorded. Your Internet service provider (cable company, phone company, etc., also called "ISP") knows every site you've visited and how long you've spent on each site.

So, remember, the Internet is NOT private. It takes great effort to make it private!

Twitter *or 'The Tweet Life'*

With the popularity of social applications like Twitter, hackers have created a whole new avenue for stealing your information and money. One of the latest attacks involves a "tweet" or Facebook post from a friend (you think) that says "Hey, check out this video." Or "Did you see this video of you?" Then the scammers post a link pointing to a site that looks exactly like Twitter or Facebook. Unsuspecting victims log on using their user id and password. What they don't realize is that the site is not actually Twitter or Facebook, but a fake redirection page, and their credentials have just been stolen. Because the thieves have been very clever so far by not using them immediately, most people never realize their credentials are compromised.

The second half of this attack involves using those credentials. They will eventually use the credentials to research people, find their friends, family, travel plans, and habits. Then they will approach the friends and family, posing as the victim to scam more information and money. Beware of tweets like "I am traveling and my wallet and credit cards were stolen. Would you wire some money to my hotel?" or "Wow, our favorite band is in town! Would you buy a couple of extra tickets and mail them to me?"

Even more insidious, they use those stolen credentials to try and hack into your other sites, figuring that if your Twitter name is 'HAPPYMONKEY15', then you might just be HAPPYMONKEY15 on Facebook, MySpace, PayPal, and others. If you are like most people, not only will your user id be the same, but so will the password (See *Passwords* section for a system of creating and remembering multiple passwords). Now, the hackers have access to additional information and maybe your real email address, which they will try as your user id for PayPal and other places where they can do real damage.

To protect yourself, teach your child not follow links from within emails, Twitter, and Facebook unless you know where they came from and who sent them to you. Even if you feel it came from a valid place, still be cautious if those links start asking for personal information like a user id and password. Be aware and careful on the web. Would your friend really be asking you those questions?

URL Shortening

Twitter often replaces link addresses with a shortened version (or a short URL). If you hover your mouse over the short URL, it SHOULD expand and show the real URL. If it expands and the link address is real, go ahead. If it doesn't expand, you are forced to ask "Why is this author hiding the real URL from me?" Some answer that Twitter forces short URLs, but that is not entirely true. URL shortening is not forced, but offered. Before you click on any link, always ask yourself, "Is this really something I need to see?" If you are running WOT (as I suggest in the *Browsers* section), it will alert you of the link's safety with a green swirl.

So your son is happily tweeting along and encounters a link to a Michael Jackson video tweeted by his best friend … he must look! Thanks to Twitter's short URL feature, and the fact that his best friend's computer had been infected with KoobFace (or the virus-of-the-week), your son's machine is now infected. Whoohooo! And a happy morning it is! Now, whenever he launches Facebook or Twitter, KoobFace will begin to send out tweets or posts as him. Those messages include a short URL that then loads KoobFace on his girlfriend's computer when she clicks on the link. So, when she starts Twitter, KoobFace tweets as her… rinse, repeat. (If your son does have the virus-of-the-week on his computer, please refer to the instructions from your antivirus software to run a scan and clean your computer.)

Twitter Usage Contract

My wife and I have determined that the potential invasiveness of Twitter merits another layer of protection with our children. We have instituted a contract that they must agree to by signing it before setting up an account.

I will be honest with you: this security measure went over like a lead balloon at our house. My popularity rating hadn't plunged so low since "Dad-the-evil" accidentally blocked Webkinz™ seven years ago. After an initial eye-roll our 15-year-old daughter took the contract to her room, read it, and soundly rejected it. My wife and I are not terribly sad about this. Until our daughter signs the contract, Twitter is one less potential portal for trouble in our household. I'm including the contract here for you to determine whether our teenager is right to refuse.

Sample Twitter Usage Contract

Date: 1/26/2015

This contract is between CHILD and PARENTS

CHILD agrees to:

- Make the Twitter account a "protected" Twitter account, and have it remain a "protected" Twitter account
- The Twitter account password must be strong and not known to anyone other than CHILD and PARENTS
- Both parent accounts will be on the approved Tweet list and remain on this list
- The "Add location to your Tweets" setting will be OFF
- "Display media that may contain sensitive content" will be OFF
- "Protect my Tweets" will be ON
- "Always use HTTPS" will be ON
- Twitter account Picture must be approved by PARENTS
- Location will remain BLANK
- Bio will be NON personal or NON identifiable and must be approved by PARENTS
- "Twitter post directly to Facebook" will remain OFF
- No applications will be approved to work with the Twitter account without approval from PARENTS
- Twitter phone app – Only approved app is the one by Twitter Inc.
- If the Twitter App is installed on the phone, the phone must be locked with a passcode that is NOT known by anyone other than CHILD and PARENTS. If the passcode becomes known, it must be changed immediately.
- The phone will have Lookout Security installed, should the Twitter App be installed.
- _____
- _____

Signed: _____ Date: _____

Google Plus Suggestions

Google+ will always share your basic profile information in a public search engine. I don't like this, so I don't have an account. If you are okay with the world being able to find you, then set up a Google Plus account. As soon as you do, head to "about" and edit the privacy settings in each area to lock them down as much as possible. The same rules as all social media apply: Don't share and keep your postings to a minimum.

Don't Share through Blogs

Blogs are great ways to learn about stuff, hear other people's opinions, and just have some fun. But our teens should remember that blogs, like everything else on the Internet, can be bad or good. Think about the blog in terms of security.

* ★ Whose blog is it?
* ★ Is the blog by a big newspaper or television station?
* ★ Or is the blog by someone you have only heard of in blogs?

Why ask? The difference may be in the fact checking. The Internet has given everyone (me included) a voice. Many people with web pages and blogs are great writers and experts in their fields. Many are not. Teach your kids to always consider the source before they act on its information.

If your teen is writing a blog, it is vital that you monitor its content, not only for appropriateness (I suspect that if you're parenting actively enough to read this far into the book, your kid has a pretty good head on his shoulders and deserves the trust that you've put into him), but more so for security issues that can arise from unintentional over-sharing. You may be able to set up your child's blog to email you whenever a new blog is posted; but some blogs require you to log on to check for recent posts.

While we are talking about blogs, we should mention Tumblr again. Tumblr is one of the most popular social media sites for teens. At this writing Tumblr boasted 223 million blogs and more than 100 billion posts. Tumblr is easy to use and offers the ability to post almost anything anyone can think up. It can be a really great place, but maybe not for young teens. Remember, on Tumblr anyone can post anything they dream up – and you may not want your kids to be exposed to some of these posts. I suggest using a contract similar to the Twitter contract above and following their Tumblr account to see what they post.

While not blog sites, sites like Wattpad provide vehicles for writing novels and sharing ideas. People from all over the world read, comment, and help craft written articles, stories, fan fiction, and poems. Wattpad requires users to be at least 13 to sign up for the site, but they can still access porn. You may want to consider a usage contract with your teen to ensure they know your expectations that they use this site strictly as a forum to express themselves creatively with other teens. If you are wondering about what your teen may be writing, you can get yourself an account (free) and read their work. You will most likely be amazed (but it is a good way to check for danger signs as well).

Social Media Do's and Don'ts

Do: Set good passwords for you social media accounts.

Don't: Do not use the same password on every account.

Do: Enjoy your social media experience safely.

Don't: Blogs are just someone's opinion. Look for the source. Where did the blog come from? Do they have fact checkers? Should you follow their advice?

Don't: Promiscuously using social media is like doing anything promiscuously: you leave yourself vulnerable to viruses.

Do: Keep your system patched.

Your Electronic Image or 'Never Email Your Anatomy'

Where did that picture come from?

DIGITAL IMAGERY IS EVERYWHERE. Every 12-year-old with a cell phone thinks that he is Ansell Adams and, sadly, every 17-year-old with a cell phone thinks that she is Suze Randall. So where do all these images go?

Digital images are forever. Once posted to any site on the Internet, they become part of recorded human history and may pop up again 30 years later. They are stored on disks on servers of services like Facebook, YouTube, MySpace, and millions of others. They are stored on the backup tapes of every service provider along the way. They are stored on the hard drives of random people's computers all over the world.

You may now be asking, "Where are you going with this? Or do you just need a Mountain Dew?"

As we move into the world of digital imagery, we can take lessons from our current batch of young Hollywood stars. Every stupid, silly picture they take or have taken at a party, in private or in public, ends up on the Internet. Do you ever get tired of seeing celebrities in their underwear? NO? Good. Because this is the beginning of an era where everywhere you are, someone will whip out a cell phone to snap a picture of you if you are doing something that seems interesting at the time.

My advice to my kids: Never let anyone take a picture of you that you don't want the whole world to see.

Sounds like common sense, doesn't it? But I am surprised every time I hear a story about someone who has emailed their anatomy to someone else. This came to my attention again just last week when my wife went "ugh, oh that is gross!" at an email. Of course, I was immediately curious. "My sister sent pictures of her husband's missing finger, and she posted them on her Facebook wall," she explained. Not the kind of questionable email content that you thought I was talking about, was it? But it's still in the realm of bad taste. His finger was removed by some tool or other at work and was looking very yucky, so, of course, her sister had to share.

If you have children, or are under 18 yourself, this is even more important. There are many cases around the nation being called "child pornography" when a minor sends a photo of their anatomy to another minor and that minor, intentionally or not, shows or sends it to someone else. In the eyes of the law, they have just traded child pornography and are now a criminal. It does not matter that the photo was sent willingly by some misguided young person, or that they were the recipient of this email. By sharing it in any way they broke the law. In one case on the East Coast, a kid was looking at a picture sent to him by his 13-year-old girlfriend in the hallway at school. His buddy, was looking over his shoulder and an administrator walked past. Being taller, he could see over the buddy and what he saw on the screen disturbed him. That poor kid, the recipient, is now listed as a sex offender in the national database. His fault? You decide. If you don't want your child to have a similar experience, talk to them! Tell them to never take or allow to have taken those kinds of pictures, never send them to anyone, and if they receive them, immediately go tell a parent or someone in authority.

The final thought on sending questionable imagery is: once sent, it is part of the permanent Internet record and could (and likely will) show up again when you least want it.

Mobile Devices or 'Lost in Space'

I HAVE TO START this chapter off with a public service announcement. Do not teach your child to text and drive. If they see you doing it, they will think it is okay for them. Talk to your child about texting and driving, and what to do if they are in a car with a friend who is texting while driving. Studies show that texting and driving impairs the driver at the same level as alcohol and drugs.

Today, almost everyone has a Smartphone, iPod, iPad, tablet, or laptop. Every one of those devices has an operating system. Every one of those devices can become infected and share your personal data with the world. Your phone or tablet device can be hacked to send your private information to bad guys on the Internet. Mobile devices need to be protected just like a computer, and because of their size and portability, even more so.

If you put all of your personal data on your phone and then lose it, your personal data is available to whoever picks it up. The same is true if you leave your iPad behind in a diner.

Two security tools will protect your mobile devices:

1. Set the screen lock on them with a code. On most devices this will be found in "Settings" under "Security", but not always. You may have to read the instructions from your manufacturer.
2. Get protection software for them. Most antivirus vendors offer a mobile product. One key feature to look for is "remote wipe". A remote wipe feature allows you to go to a website and request that your mobile device is wiped clean of your data and locked so no one else can use it. The "no one else" part is not entirely true. A good hacker can "root" or reload a device back to the original operating system and use it, but not with your data. Some protection software programs have a location service to give you the GPS location of your device so you can find it or tell the authorities.

Mobile Device Do's and Don'ts

Do: Set a screen or device lock code on all your mobile devices.

Do: Find and use security software available for your device.

Do: Turn on encryption if your device supports it.

Don't: Do not take your laptop to a bar.

Don't: Do not leave your devices unguarded while you run to the bathroom in public place.

Do: Lock your mobile devices up where you can.

Do: Be careful what data you put on your mobile device. Phones and tablets are lost more frequently than computers.

Laptops or 'Mine, Mine, Mine, Mine'

Once upon an April 12th, I received a call from Human Resources, who had a former employee on the phone who had been laid off on April 9th. HR and IT had claimed his laptop and phone from him the morning of his last day. It being a lay-off, the employee had had no warning. It seemed the ex-employee was in a panic because his tax return was on his laptop with his tax preparation software. April 15th was fast approaching and he needed his tax returns. We were actually able to accommodate him. Because his laptop had not been wiped and re-deployed, we were able to copy his files onto a CD and return them. However, if he had called a day later, the machine would have been reloaded with a fresh operating system…all of those documents would have been erased (and, don't kid yourself, if there had been any interesting documents, movies, or pictures, IT would have had a party viewing them). That same afternoon, the HR rep called me back and asked if, while I was at it, I could also copy the same ex-employee's personal photos from his laptop and his phone. Ugh.

Many people do not realize that their company laptop is actually not their personal property. Unless the company specifically tells you that they are giving you a laptop to own, the company that you work for owns it. In fact, most companies also own everything uploaded to or created on that laptop, based on some document you signed on your first day of work.

This makes company laptops less than ideal places to store personal photos, email, and tax software. Whatever you do, don't ever write the great American novel on it; your company might end up owning the rights to it!!

The Laptop Bar Song

A sad fact in today's mobile world is that laptops get left behind in bars, airports, hotel lobbies, and taxis. Laptops hate this, and the companies that own them usually get very worried about the secrets stored on them.

Little known fact: #1: Laptops don't actually like beer. That's right. They don't even drink.

Little known fact #2: Laptops like bondage.

Little known fact #3: Laptops actually become attached to their owners if they are treated well.

What do those three facts tell you?

Your laptop likes to be locked up. It doesn't care where or how, but it really likes to be locked up. You can put it in the trunk of your car (or even a rental car). You can lock it in a hotel room with a laptop lock cable. You can lock it in the hotel room safe.

Laptops are not social creatures. They are more solitary, one-on-one kind of guys. They don't like bars, and they really hate being left behind in bars. They dread the next pickup line they get, which often leads to their being interrogated and having all their secrets ripped from them or - even worse - just getting wiped so they lose their identity.

So, treat your laptop not as your drinking buddy…(Dude, I love you laptop). But treat it as your secret friend and keep it safe….. (Dude, I missed you laptop. Uh… will you hold my hair back? Uh oh).

Phones

If your children carry cell phones, you should be reviewing their call history and texting regularly.

No doubt you have heard all of the media stories about the dangers of "sexting". This is a topic you need to talk to you child about. Every month on the news we hear yet another story of some adult who gave their cell number out to an minor and ended up in trouble (or in jail) because of a text conversation with that minor. Let your child know it is safe to come to you or a trusted adult if they are the recipient of something inappropriate, and tell them NOT TO DELETE IT. And please tell them NOT to forward it to anyone, even you.

But what about the ordinary lost phone?

★ Android and Apple OS phones offer a number of protections to keep your data safe. Both let you set a passcode to open them. Set it right now.
★ Many devices let you encrypt them. If your device offers this service, do it.

With the lock code in place and the device encrypted, your data is relatively safe. I should say that your data is safe from the casual person that picks it up in a cab and thinks, "Hey, new phone, sweet!" They will be stymied by the code and go online to see if they can wipe it totally. They will not be able to register it on any major carrier and use it, if you report it to your carrier as stolen or lost.

Security software is available for both the iPhone and Android phone. There are many vendors, (Lookout, Norton, McAfee, and others) that offer packages that include safe browsing, malware detection, remote lock and remote wipe. Many include automated backup of critical information, so you can load your new device.

Tablets

Tablets are just another computer. They allow you to browse the web, watch videos, play games, and even answer email. Your tablet, just like your phone and your computer, needs protection. Set the lock code, install security software, and encrypt the data if your device allows it.

Sharing Do's and Don'ts

Don't: Do not ever post where you are going before you go or while you are there.

Do: Only post about where you have been when you are back.

Do: Assume everyone you interact with on the Internet is lying or hiding something.

Don't: Don't talk to strangers. Period. Just like the real world.

Don't: Do not use your full name and your age, your hometown, your school, your......etc. Keep the information you post to a minimum.

Don't: Never meet someone in person that you met on the Internet.

Don't: Do not post pictures or allow anyone else to post pictures of you that you would not share with your entire family. Even Grandma!

Don't: Be careful of the pictures you post. Is the setting, jacket, background giving away too much information?

Don't: Do not be mean. Don't say nasty stuff. If you cannot think of anything nice to say, just don't say anything.

Don't: Do not fall for scams. Don't respond to quizzes or surveys. Don't give them information about you.

Don't: Shortened links are dangerous. You don't know where they go. Avoid clicking on them!

Don't: In Facebook every game that you allow has access to all of your profile information, your wall, your friends, etc. Don't allow every game ever invented. Be selective. If you won't play a game again, remove it.

Don't: Don't believe everything you read on the Internet. Use your common sense. The Internet gives everyone free expression, but it doesn't filter what everyone says.

Do: Always download files from a reputable site. Paying a reputable site like Apple or Amazon for a song almost ensures you will get a clean file.

Don't: Do not visit sites that let you download something for free that you should be paying for. They are the most susceptible to have infected files loaded on them.

Don't: Do not download files illegally. This is a pathway to doom.

DO: SET UP A SAFE ENVIRONMENT

Setting Up Your Home Network or 'The Safety Dance'

SO YOU JUST GOT HOME with your new computer. The helpful employee at your local mega-mart told you that it was ready to go. You can't wait to check out Pinterest, and your kids are just about pulling out their hair to play their new computer game.

STOP!

Before your plug it into the network at your house or enter your wireless network password, just take a breath and make sure you are really ready to go on the Internet. And, yes, I said "YOUR wireless password". You do have one right? If you don't, just don't tell me. Read the section on passwords in *Let's Talk about Wireless* and then come back here.

Do not get rid of the old computer. You can reload it back to the way it came from the factory and use it as your financial computer. This is a great use of an older computer. You don't need the fastest computer on the market because most financial websites require little computer horsepower; and you only use them once or twice a week. Your old computer can be reloaded to the way it arrived at your house using the recovery instructions from the manufacturer. You can install the protection software discussed in this chapter and use this machine only for financial transactions. If you resist the urge to use it for anything else, this computer becomes a very safe tool.

As you prepare a computer for you or your child to use the Internet, there are some basics you need to know. You should install tools to keep you safe on every computer you own.

Let's set you up!

Stuff you must have before you browse:

1. Viking Helmet
2. Sword

Uh... sorry, that's another book.

OK, the real list:

Computer Security Necessities

☑ Firewall/Router

☑ DNS Resolution Service

☑ Internet Security Software

☑ Antivirus Software

☑ Reputation-based File Verification

☑ Secure Browser

☑ Sandboxed Browser

Figure 13: Computer Security Necessities

Equipped with the computer necessities listed in *Figure 13*, you can pretty much browse safely, within reason. Yes, you can still get malware (viruses, Trojans, and worms) so you must still pay attention to where you go. But you already know that.

Let's go into some detail about protections that you can install at your house.

Protecting your Internet presence starts with your basic physical network at home. Every address on the internet is scanned approximately 4 times per hour - at least. Script kiddies (junior hackers) don't care whom they are attacking, and they tell the bad guys about any successful attempts.

Your house accesses the Internet through a connection provided by your Internet service provider (ISP), be it your phone company, cable company, or maybe even a satellite company. This connection is usually in the form of a box, often called a cable or DSL modem, with their cable plugged into it and a place for you to plug in your network. Modems turn your phone or cable company's signal into Ethernet. Ethernet is the most common wired network protocol in the world. The Ethernet network cable looks like a fat phone cable.

Your network starts with the Ethernet cable that you plug into the modem. That is where your protection should begin. This is called your network edge. The components that you should use at your network edge are a router and a DNS Resolution Service. *Figure 14* depicts a typical home network.

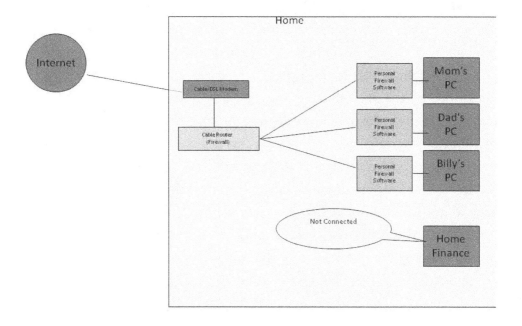

Figure 14. Sample home network diagram

Your Firewall...Your Friend

A router/firewall. Your router/firewall is wired between your modem and your computer(s). There are many companies that make cable or DSL routers, ranging in price from $20 to $1000. Most homes do fine with a unit between $60 and $200. A router is often referred to as a "firewall", but we don't want to confuse this with the firewall software that we'll be adding in *Internet Security Software*. In fact, the physical firewall is only one of the three functions that cable/DSL routers usually perform.

1. First, they connect your computers to your network. Most have at least four connections called "switch ports". They allow you to plug in multiple computers to your printer, your Smart TV, your gaming console, and your Internet service, which brings us to their second function: NAT.

2. Second, they translate the address your house is given by your cable or phone company (called your IP address) into multiple addresses, so you can use more than one computer at a time on the Internet. This second function is called "Network Address Translation" (NAT) and is performed by the firewall component of the router. This is the firewall feature that prevents people on the Internet from seeing your computers in your house, protecting you from hackers. Like its counterpart in the firefighting world, a firewall in the computer industry is a barrier device, but instead of keeping fire out, it keeps out intruders. Most firewalls are easy to use and require virtually no interaction from you. Basic units have decent firewalls (like Linksys, NETGEAR, Belkin, and Dlink) and provide enough protection for most families at home. These units cost $60 to $200. Many offer both wired and wireless connections and great speed. Be sure to match the speed of the unit to the speed that you are paying for from your Internet service provider. If you are paying for premium 50 Mb speed from your cable company, then a router that can only handle 25 Mb of traffic wastes the money you are spending on your service. Check the specs on the box or research your specs on the web first.

The unit that you purchase should have at least a basic firewall (NAT type), good for 85% of security breaches. Other more complex and business-oriented devices (i.e., Fortinet, Checkpoint, Sonicwall TZ, Watchguard), ranging between $150 - $800, offer much deeper service and are really not necessary at an average house if you install good security on each PC. These routers offer all kinds of services like antivirus, spam filtering, content filtering and many other controls. These are much harder to set up, but worth it to protect a house that is running a business (or if you are super paranoid like me!). This classification of firewall uses stateful packet inspection (SPI) and intrusion detection/prevention (IDS/IDP). This is good for 96% of security breaches.

3. The third function that many of these routers provide is wireless networking (see *Let's Talk About Wireless*). Be sure to follow your manufacturer's instructions to set up WPA2 wireless security and assign a good LONG password to connect to your house. A short password is easier to hack (more on how to select a good one in the *Don't Share: Passwords* section).

If you have only one computer you may think that you do not need a router. However, most people who own a computer also own a smartphone that can use wireless networks to save on cell data usage, or they own a tablet or iPad. If you own any other computing device at home, you will still want a router with wireless capability. Even with one computer, your router's firewall is important to protecting you and your family.

Sadly, having that hardware in your home/office does not necessarily mean that you're safe. Every time you head to the web, you are telling your firewall, "It's okay. I want to have traffic from this site to come inside my computer." Your router responds by opening the ports, and off you go. You visit your site and they send back whatever you wanted to see. Not all firewalls include traffic monitoring for viruses or other malware. The ones that offer these tools are usually more expensive. You have to manually enable those features and usually pay for the subscription that keeps them current. Even if you spring for these protections, you are still telling your firewall to open a "hole".

Security Settings on Your Firewall

★ Your new firewall/router should be set to NAT (or Network Address Translation). This is normally the default.

★ It should be set to deny any inbound traffic (also usually a default).

★ Turn on any packet-examining capabilities. Vendors call this "Deep Packet Inspection", "SPI", or anything about "packet inspection".

★ Turn on all of the "inspection" or "protection" features that your new router offers. Most of the lower-cost models do not go beyond NAT, but this is changing. Many of the lower-cost devices have features that will cause your router to examine the information sent to you from a website and determine if it is dangerous.

★ Turn on any and all antivirus, anti-spyware, malware, email filtering, spam blocking, and other protections. The more of these you can live with, the better. They will help stop all kinds of stuff from getting to your computer.

★ Content filtering: if you have kids (or a spouse who acts like one) then these settings can control the types of websites they can visit. Not all models have this, but, if yours does, take a look at these. You might like what you see. Mine, for example, blocks: hate, hacking, malware, and dangerous software sites. For the most part, it doesn't bother anyone or keep them from enjoying the Internet. There are 30 other categories that I could have chosen, as well.

★ "Logging" is another feature that many of these devices offer. This will cause your router to log activity to a computer in the house, so you can review it. If you are concerned about where your teenager is going on the Internet and worried that they are trying to hide their activity from you, then logging is your friend. Just make sure your teen does not have the password to the router or the computer used for logging. Another place that you can log activity where your teen cannot delete it is at OpenDNS.com.

There are many other settings, individual to your brand of router, so read the manual, educate yourself on these settings, and make use of them. A firewall on your network does you no good if all of the protections are turned off.

Notes for Corporate Home Users

A firewall is the best choice for every house with kids and or a business. Firewalls are more complicated than a router. If you connect to your company regularly, ask your IT networking team or helpdesk what firewalls they use at work. Find out if that vendor sells a 4th generation firewall for Home Office/Small Office. Then ask if they will help you set up a firewall at your house if you purchase the same brand they use.

Do you VPN to your company network? If so, you should also consider the same brand of firewall used by your company. Your company IT team may be able to setup a permanent VPN session between a port on your firewall and the company. This allows any computer attached to that port (or virtual Wi-Fi port) to be directly connected to the company network. Every other port on the firewall remains dedicated for home users. This takes setup skills beyond most home users and requires the IT Network team to setup and support.

DNS Resolution Service Settings on Your Firewall/Router

There are a number of services that are either free or very inexpensive that offer Domain Name Service (DNS) protection for your network. DNS is the phonebook of the Internet. Internet addresses are a string of numbers that look like "192.168.100.105". These numbers are referred to as the "IP address" of a computer. When you type www.ibm.com into your browser, your computer asks your network to translate what you typed (known as the Universal Resource Locator [URL]) into an IP address. Your network can do this automatically if you visit the site a lot and if your network hardware can store addresses (not all can). If your network does not know this address, it asks the DNS server to translate it. Your normal DNS server is located at your Internet service provider. Once your Internet service provider has translated the address, you are sent to the web page that you requested.

To protect your home network, you can tell your router to use a specific DNS server. Services like OpenDNS, Norton DNS, and Comodo Secure DNS host DNS servers that are specifically cleaned of known bad addresses. These services also allow you to choose what level of blocking you wish. Some even offer network usage reports. Setting your router to use one of these services is a good basic protection level for your home. They are all different, so read your router manufacturer's instructions on "DNS Resolution" or "DNS Service". See also the instructions on the *OpenDNS*, *Comodo Secure DNS*, or *Norton DNS* pages. OpenDNS even allows you to turn on logging, so you can track where your computers go on the Internet.

Remember my friend from the first chapter? This is the tool that defeated his son's valiant attempt to sneak onto the internet. Kids are smart. They work with computers at school. They learn from friends. As a parent, you must stay one step ahead. A DNS service with logging is a good way to monitor your child's activity. Unlike a browser's history log, without your password your child cannot change the OpenDNS log. In fact, if you don't tell your kids that you are using OpenDNS, they won't know. You can go to your OpenDNS account to see what they are doing. Tools like K9 (and many others listed later in this chapter) store your child's activity history in a separate place or on another computer so you can still see it even if they delete it.

Bandwidth and Performance Considerations

What Internet service should you subscribe to? The offers on TV, in the paper, in the mail, and online are endless. How do you choose the right speed for you?

Internet service is delivered by most carriers in different performance packages based on the speed of the connection. Most basic connections start with bandwidth between 2Mb/s and 6Mb/s (Mb/s stands for "Megabit per second" or millions of bits transmitted per second).

★ Basic cable bandwidth (2Mb/s to 8Mb/s) – Good for relatively low-use users, email, light browsing, and minimal video streaming

★ Medium: 10Mb/s to 20Mb/s bandwidth – Solid bandwidth for most people. This bandwidth range will support most connected households who watch Netflix on one or two devices at the same time, perform normal Internet work, and play some online games.

★ High speed: 30Mb bandwidth and up – These top-tier bandwidth groups are overkill for most houses, but there are some who benefit from this performance range. High bandwidth will allow for very fast downloads of big files, for a family of connected users all online at the same time, for streaming multiple videos at the same time, for playing more than one online game, and for multiple streams of video chatting (FaceTime, WebEx, Skype, etc). This range is also good for corporate users who work from home and utilize a company IP phone system and network VPN connection to the company all of the time. This range provides sufficient bandwidth so the home office worker will not impact or be impacted by other family members.

Let's Talk about Wireless...

Wireless (or Wi-Fi or a HotSpot) was designed around an international standard created to broadcast a network connection to computers. Restaurants, stores, and libraries offer "Wi-Fi" or "HotSpot" or some other name for wireless networking. Wireless networking uses radio signals to offer the same Ethernet connection to a computing device that you would otherwise get via a wire from a wall socket.

The name for a device that sends and receives wireless Ethernet signals is an "access point" or AP. Almost every cable/DSL router you buy today is also an "access point" or AP. Wireless networking means that your laptop can use your home's network connection to your ISP without a cable. If you are like me and have computers in more than one room, you can save yourself the expense (and ugliness) of running cables all over your house by setting up wireless networking.

Remember that wireless networking also means that your signal travels outside your house where someone else may pick it up. Before you use your wireless network, be sure to follow the suggestions in the *Set Up Instructions* for *Wireless Sample Set-Up*. Your iPod, iPad, tablet, Kindle Fire, and Barnes and Noble Nook all require a wireless network to connect to the Internet. Many phones can become "Hotspots" and offer wireless Ethernet connections for computing devices.

You probably have a wireless network in your house. Most people these days do. Do you mind sharing it with all your neighbors? Why not be a nice neighbor and let anyone within 300 feet freely use your wireless network? It does seem neighborly… but it will seem less neighborly when (1) that neighbor's kid interferes with your system's performance by running an intense on-line role-playing game across your network; or when (2) the FBI shows up at your house to take your computers as evidence and arrest you as the responsible party because that same neighbor-kid was using your wireless network to perpetrate a crime. Imagine your entire carefully gathered stamp collecting materials (wink wink, nudge nudge) gone in a bad federal suit flash.

One day, I was sitting in our computer room (ex-dining room), upgrading my router, when my wife said, "Hey, I was just looking at the weather on Weather.com, and I think we going to have rain soon." To which I answered "Uh huh" and went back to the firmware update of the router which was at 35%.

Then I paused. "Honey, did you say you were on the Internet?"

"Yes," she answered.

I looked back at my screen. 60%. Uh oh. "Are you using your tablet?" I asked.

"Yes, why?"

I paused here. "Well, the network is down. What network are you using?"

At this point we realized that her tablet had discovered that our network was down and switched to the next strongest available network. This is not good.

When you turn on your computer at home and start the wireless, how many wireless networks do you see? I live in a fairly normal suburban neighborhood, and I see ten from my easy chair. Of ten networks that I could connect to, eight are protected with a password. Eight! Yep, in my recliner, I could connect to two different networks. I won't, because that is illegal. But not everyone is honest.

If you take your new wireless router out of the box and turn it on, it will broadcast wireless to every computer within range (approximately 100 to 300 feet). Everyone who can receive that signal can connect to it and use your Internet connection. In fact, the way most operating systems are set up, they will use the strongest signal over any weaker signal. At my house in my bedroom, my neighbor's wireless signal is stronger than mine (which is in my basement, two floors below). My laptop would much rather connect to his network if I let it.

What should you do? Here is a list of basics

★ Rename your router: All of the new routers from the major manufactures (Linksys, Belkin, NETGEAR, etc.) have start-up programs to get you up and going as quickly as possible. Use these. Most are on a CD that you put in your computer and run. These programs guide you through the basics of setting up your new router securely, including giving it a name. Why give it a name? You want to distinguish it from the networks that belong to neighbors who also bought your brand of router and did not rename theirs.

★ Stop the broadcast of the SSID. The SSID is the name of your wireless network that your router calls out to the world every few seconds so computers can find it. Turn it off. By doing this, computers will only connect to your network if they are specifically told to by a person.

★ Start WPA2 (wireless encryption). This requires that you choose a password and tell your wireless router and your computer what that password is. Only computers with the password will be able to connect to your network AND – and this is a big AND – this is the only way you will stop anyone with a wireless card from reading your traffic. If you don't turn this setting on, your traffic is traveling the airwaves in clear text, meaning that anyone who wanted could see everything you send to the Internet, even your credit cards and passwords. In the Set Up Instructions, Wireless Sample Set Up shows sample settings on a NETGEAR N300 router.

Internet Security Software

You need a separate Internet security/ antivirus software package on your computer, in addition to the hardware you just bought. There are many packages available, ranging from very good free ones to very good consumer versions. Many cable/phone/local Internet service providers offer free security software. Check with your cable company or phone company to see if they offer a free security product for being their customer. Whichever you choose, install one and keep it up to date.

Internet security packages like Norton Security, McAfee Internet Security, and Comodo Internet Security, and many others usually include antivirus and firewall software. Comodo Firewall is a standalone firewall you can install separately if you purchase an antivirus software package that comes without a firewall. Your Windows operating system even came with one; but it is better to use the one that came with your Internet security package.

When you have your Internet security package running, you still have some responsibility to pay attention to it when it asks you "Hey! Should I allow this?" When this happens, you need to read the message and respond. Packages from Norton, McAfee, and others make most decisions for you.

These messages are important! If you always say "yes", you are making your Internet security software useless. If you click on the wrong option, you will need to open your antivirus software and adjust the settings:

★ to allow something you've just blocked,
★ to disallow something you didn't block,
★ make an action a one-time allow or block, or
★ set a permanent allow or block.

Antivirus / Anti-Spyware

Normally bundled with your Internet security software, antivirus / anti-spyware examines files that you move to and from the Internet and those already on your computer to determine whether they contain malware. You should set your antivirus / anti-spyware:

★ to always be active (usually termed "real time mode"),
★ to scan your machine every day, and
★ to update itself with the latest Internet threats every day.

There are many good antivirus products. My favorites include: Norton, McAfee, Comodo, Trend Micro, AVG, Immunet, BitDefender, and Avast.

Through most of this book I talk about computers running Microsoft Windows. If you are running a Macintosh from Apple, do not discount the need for an antivirus suite. You should still definitely run one. If you are a Linux user, then you don't have many antivirus options, but you can and should turn on your firewall and add some useful extensions or add-ons to your browsers. See _Browsers_ section.

Be careful. Buy your antivirus from a reputable seller! Fake antivirus software is a common scam. Virtually everyone who browses the Internet will see this message at some time: "Your system is infected!" says the blinking orange box. "Just click here to fix it." Please don't click on it. It will only lead you to one of two places.

- ★ Best case: they install a root kit on your system that turns it into a zombie used to attack their next major corporate target (or, shudder, their next government target). This is how my sister-in-law became introduced to some very unhappy Italian government officials. A website that she'd set up for her small business was hijacked and used to attack the Italian government. By the time she was contacted, there was nothing she could do but shut it completely down. Each month we send her monthly care packages with her favorite tea and cigarettes that she can barter with the other orange jump-suited women.

- ★ Worst case: they install a root kit on your system that turns it into a zombie used to attack their next major corporate target and steals all of your private information at the same time.

What do you do?

NEVER click on one of those links.

Simply close the pop-up window. The best way to close a pop-up window is <u>not</u> by clicking on the "X" in the upper right corner. Some particularly clever scams hide links or commands that will damage your computer under a fake "X" in the corner of the pop-up. Instead, head to the bottom of the screen. Hover your mouse over the browser icon on the bar (*Figure 15*).

Figure 15: Pop-up on start bar

When you do this, Windows will show you a miniature version of the browser window. (*Figure 16*) When you hover over this miniature version, a small red "x" will appear in the right corner (the "x" will not appear until you hover over the box). Click the "x" that corresponds to the pop up. (see the orange arrow in *Figure 16*). This will safely close the pop up window.

Figure 16: Pop-up showing red X

After you've closed the box, run a virus scan. If it comes up clean, you are probably okay.

Reputation Based File Verification

A reputation based file verification tool is a great addition to any computer. These are Internet-based tools that will check files you are opening or downloading against a database of known files on the Internet. These are excellent at catching viruses that are too new for the normal antivirus systems to catch. If your file matches a known 'good' file, the tool will do nothing. If the file matches a known 'bad' file the tool will block you from downloading it and tell you. If the file does not match any known file, the tool will let you know and give you the option of continuing. If you are sure that this file is safe (it came from your work, or school, or someplace you trust), download it. (Note: Your antivirus tool will scan it for viruses when it has completed downloading). Reputation based file verification tools add on to your existing antivirus tool. I personally use either Immunet or ThreatFire for this job. Both are free at this time.

Configuration of Your Computer (Not Your Child's)

Windows-based PC users need to perform some basic setup configurations on your computer before venturing out into the wide world of the Internet. Sample settings for a parent's computer using MS Windows are outlined step-by-step in the *Set-Up Instructions* section.

Do's and Don'ts of Setting Up Your Computer

Do: Set the computer to check for updates automatically.

Do: Set a strong password on the computer and on each account.

Do: The first thing you should do when you get a new computer is install your Internet security software (Norton, McAfee, Trend, Zone Alarm, Comodo, et al.).

Do: Make sure your Internet security software has the firewall enabled.

Do: Make sure your Internet security software has the active malware protection enabled.

Do: Make sure your Internet security software is set to automatically update itself.

Do: Install your favorite secure browser. (detailed in *Secure Browsers*).

Don't: Unlike you would set up your child's computer, you will not want the browser on your adult computer to record your browsing history, save passwords, or save cookies. These settings leave your information vulnerable to hackers and scammers. For very young children, you may want to enable these as conveniences, as their activities shouldn't lead a hacker to your financial information.

Do: Install your sandbox software.

Do: Install your link scanner (AVG Linkscanner, McAfee Siteadvisor).

Do: Install your reputation based file verification (Immunet, Threatfire).

Don't: Do not browse the Internet widely until you have completed the above steps.

Do: Use an older computer you have rebuilt just for banking, shopping, taxes and other financial work. Everybody upgrades their computer eventually; keep the old one. Reload the operating system following the manufacturer's instructions, load it with security tools, and use it only for your private work.

Do: Set an administrator password on the computer (your parent account).

Configuration for a System for Kids

Still want to go to the Internet after hearing about all of the dangers and pit falls? Of course you do and so do your kids! After considering the nearly endless supply of research, financial, and entertainment options that the Internet offers, most parents determine that the potential benefits outweigh the possible risks. To minimize those risks, we can apply some general strategies.

You already know to always supervise your kids when they are using the Internet. In our house, we have arranged the family computers so that we can see them from the kitchen when cooking or living room when sitting. My wife and I have our "Internet Computers" in the same room so we are there with the kids on the Internet. This way we are the ultimate "alpha browsers" in our household, monitoring everything our children see.

The Internet contains stuff that no one needs to see or, at the very least, that many people find offensive. Teach your children how to search safely on the Internet. Many schools have safe search engines that they encourage their students to use. Contact your child's school and find out about their web resources. My kids had access to our school district web resources from as early as first grade.

Build a kid-safe environment for using the Internet. First, you need to set your child's computer browser to use "safe search" as the search method so if you or your children are searching for a topic you won't get bombarded with stuff that may be inappropriate or even offensive. I give instructions on how to set this in *Locking Safe Search Mode*.

If you have a home network, you should be using one of the DNS (Domain Name Service) protections from companies like Norton, OpenDNS, and Comodo. These services protect your entire network starting at the edge (your router) by checking the sites you are visiting against a safe sites list, so your child won't browse to known malware or identity theft sites. Detailed instructions for finding and setting up this protection are found for setting up three different DNS Resolutions Services in the *Set-Up Instructions* section.

Normally, I would tell you that you need to protect your privacy further by setting your browser to NOT remember history. But, since we are setting up this system to protect your children, you want to leave 'history' on. In fact you should review that history regularly to see what they are doing.

You should still tell websites that you do not want them to track your activities. This ensures that websites (the ones that are following the rules) will not record your child's activity. You should know that many websites do not follow these rules, so this precaution, while a very good thing to set, cannot be relied only solely.

Even if you implement these privacy settings, the places that you visit may still be watching you. Most people believe that Facebook and others will record all of the sites that you visit if you open another tab on your browser while you have Facebook open. Facebook claims that they no longer do this, but the fact that they did at one time should tell you that the technology to do this is available to any website you visit. To be safe, before you start doing things that you want to keep private (like banking, shopping, or other stuff), you should close and start a new browser.

Not everything you have set up for your parental computer is appropriate for a child's machine. Sample settings for a child's computer using MS Windows are outlined step-by-step in the *Set-Up Instructions* section. If you followed the instructions in the previous section, you have already set the password for your parent account and the system administrator. Because this account will be the only one that can actually change your system (install software, add user accounts, etc.) the account and its password should be kept secret from the kids. You will need User Accounts for each child. Be sure to tell everyone in the family to "Logoff" their accounts when they are done each day.

If you wish, you can use Microsoft Parental Controls, install Microsoft Live Family Safety, or install K9 to control how long a particular account can use the computer each day or even what programs they can run and not run. K9 from Bluecoat also provides monitoring and protection. I talk about this product in detail under _Content Filtering_. For any child under the age of 15, I highly recommend this product. In the case of a younger child, you can disallow all browsers other than the kid-safe one that you installed (see _Kids Browsers_), forcing them to use only the safe ones. If you install K9, this is less necessary, but the Kidoz environment and browser are really kind of fun! Using K9, Microsoft Parental Controls, or any of the commercial child protection tools (i.e. NetNanny), you can control programs and games installed on the computer by name or rating. More detailed information on these controls can be found in _Tools for Monitoring Your Child_.

Do's and Don'ts of Setting Up Your Child's Computer

Do: All of the same "Do's" for an adult computer apply here, except...

Don't: Do not set your child's browser to clear history. You'll want to review this regularly.

Do: Install a protection and monitoring program (K9, Microsoft Live Family Safety, NetNanny).

Do: Set the browser to Safe Mode.

Do: Set up accounts for each child to use the computer.

Do: Remind them to go to the Start Menu and "Logoff" when they are done.

Do: Consider setting up Windows Parental Controls for your kid's account.

Browsers or "Who's Browsing Whom?"

THE OTHER DAY I walked into my oldest child's bedroom and she quickly shut the lid to her laptop. Immediate danger sign! So, I had to take the machine and open it back up. Expecting the worst, I was confused to be faced with Webkinz™, a children's game site associated with her favorite stuffed animals <u>and</u> on our list of approved sites. It took me a moment to recover, but then I had to ask my teenager, "Why shut the lid to the computer?"

"You told us the rule was 'no Internet in our rooms behind closed doors'." Whew! She broke the rule, but why do I feel like I dodged a bullet?

In a nutshell, here are my do's and don'ts for browsing the Internet (these rules are applicable to adults, as well as children):

Don't: Don't click on pop-up ads or fall for a "contest" that you see advertised on the side of your browser window (or anywhere else on the site).

Don't: Don't visit most Internet-based gambling sites.

Don't: Unless you trust the merchant or website, don't give them information about you or your credit cards, bank account, social security number, etc. How do you know if you should trust them? There are a number of ways. First: do you know the business? If you regularly shop in their brick and mortar store, then there is a high probability that they are safe. If they don't have a store, like Amazon.com, but they are reputable, they will be listed by the Better Business Bureau (www.bbb.org). You can also look at the Web of Trust or Norton Safe Surf rating (most Internet security software packages have something similar).

Do: Before entering personal information, look for the "lock" on your browser. Usually it is located next to the website address at the top of the page (see *Figure 17*). If it signifies "locked", you are safer typing in personal information. The lock tells you that your browser is set up for encrypted traffic, so no one can intercept your personal information while you are sending it. Another way to tell is to check the address on the address bar. Most browsers will show the change of address from HTTP: to HTTPS:. To determine whether or not you are on a secure site, a simple way to remember is to think HTTPS: "S" for "secure".

Figure 17: HTTPS and "the lock"

My wife was trying to buy a book. We went to a major bookstore's online website and found the book. She put the book into her cart and clicked on "Checkout". When the checkout screen appeared she looked for the lock on the address bar before she started typing our address and credit card information. It wasn't there. The page wasn't locked. We both looked at the screen and wondered, "Hmmm, what now?" We tried closing and re-loading the checkout screen, but there was still no lock. We closed the browser and tried a different one. No lock. We decided to wait on our purchase. A few days later my wife tried the site again and, sure enough, there was the lock. Whew. She completed her purchase and became the happy owner of another book.

Do: Before entering any personal information, ask yourself, "Why do they want / need this information?" and "Does it make sense, based on what I'm visiting their site for?"

Do: Read their privacy policy (required to be easy to find by law).

Browsers

Computer geeks (I am one) are the same everywhere. The other day at work I walked in on a heated argument, with mouths foaming, spittle, large arm gestures, and shouting. At first, I thought the two were going to come to blows; then I wondered why the other two in the room didn't break them up. You can understand how they became so emotionally charged. Just listen to what they were saying:

"Opera™ is so faster than Chrome™."

"Yah, well, Chrome™ has solid security, and Opera is written by the Chinese KGB to spy on you."

"Really and you trust Google®? They don't sell all your search information to anyone who pays?"

To which one of the bystanders said quietly, "I think Firefox™ is the best…"

At which point I backed out of the room as quietly as I entered.

Before we get to browsers, the conversation above was real but not correct. To the best of my knowledge, Opera (which is a browser) was not written by the Chinese to spy on us.

A browser is a program that you can install on your computer that allows you to visit (or browse) the World Wide Web (WWW) or what most people think of as the Internet. There are three major players in the browser market (and a number of smaller ones). The most common browsers are:

* **Firefox**™, is an excellent security-minded browser and it is free. Install the WOT (Web of Trust) add-on before you browse. If you really want it to be secure, install the add-on called "no-script". This will let you control any program (or script) that someone wants to run on your computer. This is a very cool tool.
* **Google Chrome**™. This browser is also very security-minded and free. Again, you will want to install the WOT extension before you browse.
* **Microsoft's Internet Explorer (IE) 9** is the best Microsoft browser for security purposes. Be sure to patch it every time Microsoft releases a high or critical patch. WOT is also a good add on to this browser.

New Security Browsers

A new breed of browser is emerging on the market specifically designed to protect your identity, your privacy, and your safety on the Internet. Referred to as "security browsers" or "privacy browsers", these browsers are great for you, the adult. However, they may not be great for your kids, because they block, re-route, and obfuscate all browsing patterns, making it no longer possible for you to track your kids' activity on the Internet. You can remedy this by installing parental software on their computers. If you wish to keep track of what your children are browsing, then use a kids' browser (see *Specialized Browsers for Kids*). If your child is older and your concerns are limited to safety rather than "nannying", you can have them use a privacy browser. These browsers eliminate the need for the add ons and extensions mentioned in *Extensions and Add ons*. The most popular security browsers are:

* **Epic Browser** – a private browser project backed by some big players in the computing world, this browser protects your privacy on the Internet. One unique feature of Epic is its ability to encrypt your Internet path from the browser on your desktop to your Internet endpoint, effectively blocking your location. Some people will be confused initially when they see websites interpreting their location

to be in other countries. This is part of how they obscure your identify. Otherwise, your browsing should remain consistent.

★ **Comodo Ice Dragon** – (a Firefox based privacy browser), **Comodo Dragon** (a Chrome-based privacy browser), and **Comodo Chromium Secure** (a Chromium-based browser), all offer a variety of layers to secure your privacy. You may find it beneficial to visit www.comodo.com to compare their features directly.

Browsing is still most secure when you use your own common sense. If you (or your children) browse sites of a questionable nature, you risk a higher chance of infection. Think before you browse.

Questionable sites include:

★ Gambling
★ Hacking
★ Hate and Anarchy
★ Illegal Activities
★ Pornography

Extensions and Add-ons

Add-ons are like the dealer-added-options on a new car. They are neither part of the original car nor made by the manufacturer, but they make your experience better and safer.

To make sure you have the safest browsing experience possible, you need to install extensions (in Chrome™) or Add-ons (in Firefox™) that will also protect you.

WOT

One of the best is WOT or "Web of Trust". This add on / extension for Chrome™ and Firefox™ gives you an indication of the safety of the sites in your search results by showing a green, yellow, or red circle next to each site. Sites with poor reputations will have red circles next to them. You should avoid those sites. The add-on / extension will also put up a warning page if you click on a red site, giving you the option to go back or to go to the site against their advice. Listen to them: don't go there!

Interesting story here, even your intrepid author needs the tools he talks about in this book. All of my browsers have WOT and Norton Safe Web running. I was reviewing the list of links to information for parents when one of them was marked with a red circle by WOT. I thought, "Odd." That is a very reputable company, and they are still in business. It turned out I had simply put a typo into my list of links. I never go directly to a web page that I don't visit every day. On this occasion I had typed the name into my search bar and the result showed with a red circle. When I corrected the typo, the results were marked with a green circle.

The other possibility would be that the reputable vendor's website had been compromised. This actually happens to professionals, not just ordinary people. Security vendors are great targets for hackers. If they can break into and take over the web page of a security company, they get bragging rights forever. You have a pretty good chance of avoiding fake and compromised pages if you run the tools mentioned in this book. If WOT had not caught this page, OpenDNS might have, or Norton, which is why I run more than one tool.

Symantec's Norton and McAfee's Internet Safety Antivirus and Internet Safety tools both have their own reputation monitors which work similarly to WOT. If you have either of these tools - and I highly recommend either of them - you should still run WOT for added protection. *A Sample Set Up for WOT* is included in *Set Up Instructions*.

Sandboxing Your Browser

Sandboxie is an inexpensive tool that confines all of your browsing activity inside a virtual "sandbox" and away from the rest of your computer. Using a sandbox will stop many threats that get past all of the other tools listed above. I have it installed on all of our family browsing computers. We have learned that some of the more complex game functions are not allowed in the sandbox.

Ever heard of Webkinz™? My girls love them. Sandboxie does not. I became "Dad the Evil" very quickly in my house when I zealously installed Sandboxie on every computer. Webkinz™ stopped working. It was bad. I had to set up a non-sandboxed browser just for this program. We have found that Google Chrome™, a browser with a built-in sandbox, seems to work well with these games. Or, if you are looking for a free home-use Internet Security Suite, the Comodo Internet Security Suite collection is good and includes sandboxes.

Don't even ask me about when my sandbox interfered with my wife's Yoville game. Some security improvements can cost you your happy home!

Link Scanner

Link scanners look at all the links on the webpage you are visiting and determine whether they are part of a database of known safe sites or known dangerous sites. The most common scanners are AVG LinkScanner and McAfee Site Advisor. Both are free. Norton Security and Norton 360 include a link scanner as well.

System Cleaner

A system cleaner is probably overkill for a kid's computer, unless you are going to be using it for your financial information. A system cleaner is a great additional tool that I run on my financial and browsing computer. On a weekly, monthly, or manual basis, they clean your computer of your Internet history; look for and remove private information stored by websites (in cookies); check and clean the registry; and keep the hard drive clean of junk. They are great tools for keeping your computer running well. I use Comodo System Utilities, but CCleaner by Piriform and System Cleaner by Pointstone have good reviews.

Other Extensions and Add-ons

Other great extensions and add-ons are Ad Block Plus, Better Privacy and (for the really paranoid browser like me) Firefox™ with NoScript add-on running. NoScript actually stops most web pages from working and annoys a lot of people. Personally, I love it! This add-on creates a button on the bottom right of the screen that lets you choose which services on the web page to allow.

This feature will amaze you. If we use Best Buy as an example, the button will appear when we navigate to the page. Clicking it gives you the option to allow www.bestbuy.com to run "always", "this session", or "never". Since we trust Best Buy, we click "always". If you look for a specific product, the button re-appears. Click on it and you may find that Monetate.net and Doubleclick.net both want to run. Huh? I thought we were at the Best Buy website. We are, but, like most companies, Best Buy uses web services from other vendors for their website. Doubleclick is an ad populating and gathering service (in other words, they are responsible for the ads that run along the right side of the web page). I am not interested in those ads, especially since they are outside of Best Buy's control, so I leave that one blocked. Monetate is something I have not heard of, so for now it stays blocked. This is a good rule of thumb, but if the page does not work right, you will have to allow things to run for this session. This can be somewhat annoying, but if you give them temporary approval you can always shut down the browser and restart to clear your settings. By the way, your "always" settings are remembered by NoScript.

Kids' Browsers

One evening my youngest asked me to help her with her homework. She had to write a report (in early junior high school) on the Greek goddess Aphrodite. Seemed simple enough. She had a school-approved website to go to for the information, but she wanted a picture of the goddess for her poster. No problem, right? I opened my browser and headed to my favorite search engine. I keyed in "Aphrodite", clicked " images", and *!#@*#!!!!! Wow! I quickly hit the back button before my youngest could see the results. Thank the stars I had not had her run the search. To solve this, we headed back to the website that her school recommended and used the search engine there. Much better! Animated and kid-safe pictures appeared. Whew.

There are special browsers that you can install on your kids' computer like Kido'z (which can be downloaded from www.kidoz.net). This browser regulates which sites they can go to, forces safe searching, and has parental controls to customize the browser.

AOL also has a great environment for kids. Once you have set up the parent's account, you can set up the kids' accounts and input their ages. When they start AOL to browse or email, they get an AOL kids' account, which features a special, safe environment for kids.

Kids.yahoo.com is another site that you can set as your normal browser. It, too, restricts what kids can get to on the Internet by using a safe search engine by Yahoo. In _Tools for Monitoring Your Children_, I talk more about resources for parents monitoring and protecting their kids.

Safe Searching

A great safe searching website for kids is www.safesearchkids.com which is hosted by Google. This site uses the Google search engine with the maximum safe settings set automatically and no way to remove them.

Yet another site for slightly younger kids is www.kidsclicks.org which is run by Google. This site also forces the safe search option of the Google search engine to be on for the session.

On your own, make sure your kids' browsers are set to use "Safe Search" mode on their default search engine. The Google search engine allows you to set it to "strict safe search" mode and lock it there with a password. This will return cleaner results for your children's searching. _Steps for Locking Safe Search Mode_ are included in _Set Up Instructions_.

When the Safe Search lock is on, the top of the search results page looks different in two ways: 'Safe Search is locked' is displayed below the search box, and colored balls appear on the right. The results page is designed to look different enough that you can immediately tell whether the lock is on or off – even from across the room.

The Google Family Safety Center is a great place to start learning about searching. Visit it at http://www.google.com/goodtoknow/familysafety/.

Content Filtering and Controlling What They Can Access

My wife does a lot of online research from our home, so we've set up her work computer to be less stringent than the children's. Sadly, I had installed content filtering for all of our computers at the router initially, but was encouraged by my wife to adjust these settings when she was blocked from researching "breast cancer" for her hospital client.

There are two places you can control content on your home network. What do I mean by controlling content? I am talking about blocking access to sites that you don't want your family to access. The most basic form of blocking will block sites that are known to contain viruses, other malware, or scams that can harm you. From there you can adjust your blocking to include things like pornography, gambling, hate, etc. All blocking can be done on the actual computer (which is great for setting up a kid-specific computer with very tight restrictions); OpenDNS (which blocks the website at your network edge); or at the network, usually at the router / firewall (which is great for general protection from known bad sites).

You can install software on your computer to help you keep track of what the kids are doing and protect them even if they accidentally stray from your safe browsing environment.

My favorite is **K9** by Blue Coat Security. The K9 software will block websites in more than 70 categories, including pornography, gambling, drugs, violence / hate / racism, malware / spyware, and phishing. It forces

Safe Search on all major search engines and lets you set restrictions to block web access during designated times (Are they sneaking onto the Internet after bedtime? Not anymore!). Parents can configure custom lists for "always allow" and "always block". Another nice feature is that parents can override a web page block with password. This is particularly useful if your child is researching something that the software may misinterpret as less than benign, like breast cancer. The software has built-in tamper prevention to keep kids from shutting it down. Reports allow parents to monitor and review web activity and then adjust the controls if required. This software is compatible with Windows or Mac machines.

Microsoft has a package called **Family Safety** which is similar to K9 but not quite as complete. The main difference is in the Windows accounts on the computer. Adult accounts are not monitored and blocked, while children's accounts are. It works with multiple computers, so all are set up the same way and the reports are combined by user.

Bsecure and **NetNanny** are two of the highest recommended paid-for software packages for keeping kids safe on the Internet. Both have mobile software for Apple and Android-based phones.

Tools to Protect Adults while on the Internet

If you are more concerned about searching on the Internet and stopping every connection vendor along the way from seeing your results, you can set your browser to use Google's SSL Searching. This service sets up an encrypted session between your browser and Google, so no one in between can see your searches.

Google's SSL browsing is available at https://www.google.com or https://encrypted.google.com. You can set it to be the default search engine in your browser. The critical difference in the Google URL is the "s" in the "https". That "s" tells the web server you are accessing, to encrypt your session. Sample settings for Google SSL are included in *Set Up Instructions*.

Now that you have secured your browsing, you should check that your "safe search" settings on your browser of choice are either strict or moderate. Both will protect you from seeing the worst of the Internet.

Setting Up Your Environment Do's and Don'ts

Do: Make the Internet a family activity, so you can teach your children good Internet behavior.

Do: Install a cable / DSL router at your house between your Internet hookup and your computers. _Chapter: Setting Up Your Home Network_

Do: Turn on all of your Cable / DSL Router firewall features came with. _Chapter: Setting Up Your Home Network_

Do: Secure your wireless with a strong password. _Chapter: Setting Up Your Home Network_

Don't: Give out your wireless password to anyone. Change your password regularly and use a "guest wireless" if you need to let others on your network. _Chapter: Setting Up Your Home Network_

Do: Set up a DNS Resolution service like OpenDNS, Comodo Secure DNS, or Norton DNS. If you use Comodo or OpenDNS, set up the parental controls and logging! _Chapter: Stay Involved_

Do: Set your browser to "do not track me".

Do: Set your search engines to "safe search".

Do: Contact your child's school and find out about their web resources.

Do: Use a good browser with the security options turned on. Firefox™ and Chrome™ are considered more secure by many security industry professionals.

Do: Set your kids computers up with safe browsers like Kidoz or AOL set in kid-mode.

Do: Watch for warning signs including a browser with NO history, the suspicious closing of the laptop, or kids quickly clicking the mouse key when you walk in. *Chapter: Stay Involved*

Don't: Do not overdo content filtering on the adults' computers. When your wife is working under a tight deadline, this can turn her computer into the equivalent of a useless brick that she may consider launching at your head. I speak with the voice of experience.

Do: Install a good antivirus. Purchase one from a reputable source. (i.e. Norton, McAfee), or get one free with Comodo Internet Security. Free is good, but, frankly, Norton is always at the top of the tests (and is only around $50 a year). *Chapter: Setting Up Your Computer*

Do: Work with your kids on the Internet as they grow. Make the Internet a family event. *Chapter: Safe Internet Behavior*

Do: Install child protection on your child's PC. K9 by Bluecoat is a great free tool. In the *Stay Involved* chapter I mention others. *Chapter: Stay Involved*

Do: Get Minor Monitor if you allow your child to have a Facebook and/or Twitter account. *Chapter: Stay Involved*

Top 3 Do's and Don'ts

LET'S PUT IT ALL TOGETHER. Throughout the book I gave strategies to prepare parents to help keep their children and families safe on the Internet. Here is a recap of the top Do's and Don'ts that every parent should be doing.

1. **Do**: Stay involved. Setting your family up to safely explore the Internet is not a one-time, turn-key operation. By making the Internet a family event and working with your kids, side-by-side, parents can set Internet rules, and model good Internet behaviors. Ultimately, parents need to know and watch for warning signs that children may be straying into dangerous territory (like when the browser has no history or kids close the laptop or quickly click the mouse key when you walk in).

2. **Don't**: Do NOT share! This seems opposite to what we've been teaching our kids since they were out of their cribs, but the path to Internet disaster is lined with good intentions and over-sharing. Children need to know that sharing passwords is not okay. Parents need to know how to keep from accidentally sharing their wireless networks. Everyone needs to know the critical dangers of sharing too much information on their social media sites.

3. **Do**: Set up a safe environment. Tons of tools are available to ensure your family's safe use of the Internet. One key piece of equipment that you'll need can actually be held in your hands: a router that can protect your family with a firewall. You'll also need reputable software for antivirus, child protection, activity monitoring, and more in-depth internet security services.

SET UP INSTRUCTIONS OR 'STEP BY STEP BY STEP'

Wireless Sample Set Up

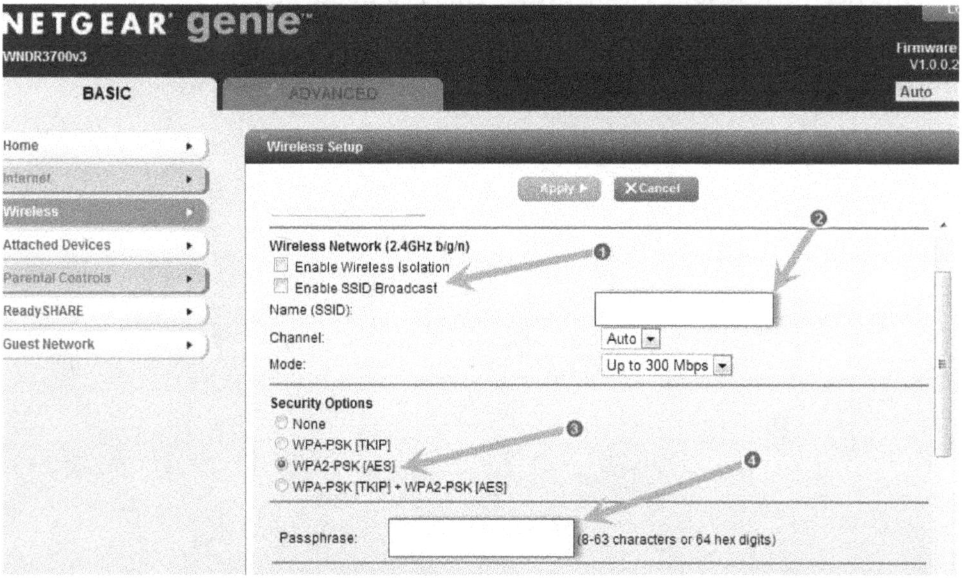

Figure 18. Sample settings on a NETGEAR N300 router.

When you set up your router's wireless, there are some basic settings you want to make sure you have set. In *Figure 18* above, *Arrow #1* shows that the "SSID Broadcast" box is NOT checked. By choosing not to enable SSID broadcasting, you can hide your home's wireless network from computers that have not been told the name of your network. You will have to manually enter the SSID of your network into your computers so they can find it.

Arrow #2 points to the box where you will fill in the SSID (name) of your home wireless network. Use any name you like, just don't leave it blank. An unnamed network will use the manufacturer's default name. Skipping the SSID name could cause confusion if your neighbor uses the same brand router and also relies on the manufacturer's default name.

Under "Security Options" (*Arrow #3*), you should select "WPA2". Manufacturers have different names for WPA2 (WPA2 Personal, WPA2 Home, or WPA2+PSK), but they are all the same. Do not choose WPA2 Enterprise.

Arrow #4 is pointing to the box where you will type in the password that every computer, tablet, or mobile device will need to access your home wireless network. This password should be strong. An example is: "This is my home network 434321 Password!" This is a good, strong password, using capital letters, numbers, and special characters. Your router may offer more security settings.

Norton DNS Example

To sign up for the free Norton DNS service, go to https://dns.norton.com

Click on "Home User" and agree that you are a home user. You will be presented with a box with three options: security (malware, phishing sites and scam sites); security + pornography; or security + pornography + non-family friendly.

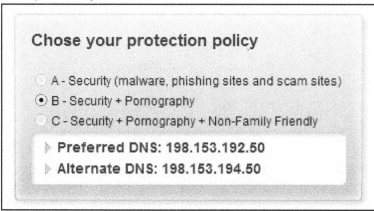

Figure 19: Norton DNS Router Settings

Select A, B, or C, based on the protection that you wish. The page displays the IP addresses for the DNS service you have chosen. You will need to program these IP addresses into your router at home.

To do this, you need to access your router by typing in the IP address that you assigned to it when you installed it into your network. Usually it looks like 192.168.1.1 or 192.168.0.1. Sign in and follow the instructions to access the DNS settings screen. *Figure 20* shows the DNS settings screen on a Sonicwall TZ210. Your router will have a similar screen or setting. Refer to your instructions, or you can use the instructions on the https://dns.norton.com.

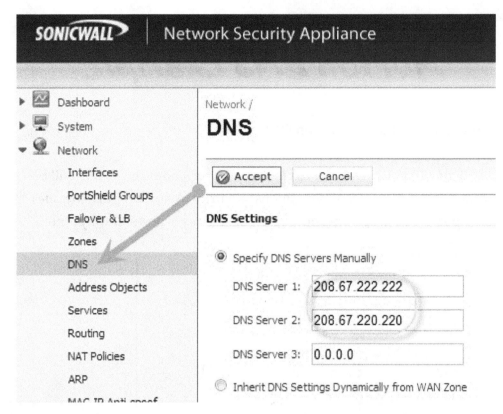

Figure 20: Sonicwall DNS Router Settings

OpenDNS or Comodo Sample Set Up

OpenDNS and Comodo Secure DNS add a very strong layer of protection to your Internet activity and are free for the basic service. Setting up OpenDNS is easy. If you love it like I do, their $20 a year premium service is a good investment. These instructions are for OpenDNS, but setting up Comodo Secure DNS is very similar.

As I mentioned earlier, OpenDNS will check every URL typed into a browser or from any application and make sure it is going to a safe, valid site. The service can also block pornography and other bad sites.

Your first step is to visit their website: www.opendns.com

Go to their home user section by selecting "For Home" (*Figure 21*).

THE LARGEST INTERNET-WIDE SECURITY NETWORK.

OpenDNS protects 2% of the Internet's active users every day, enabling the world to connect with confidence on any device, anywhere, anytime.

For Business   For Home

Figure 21: Open DNS Home Selection

From Home Solutions click the "Get Started" button (*Figure 22*).

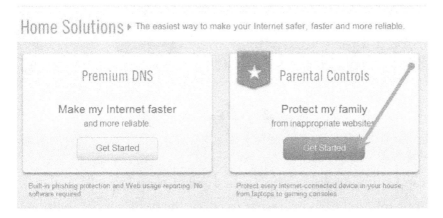

Figure 22: Open DNS – Get Started Choices

There are three selections here. The easiest is the pre-configured OpenDNS FamilyShield. Click "Sign Up Now" for OpenDNS FamilyShield to set up a free protection package pre-configured for parents that blocks all adult content (*Figure 23*).

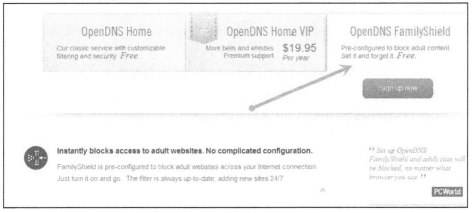

Figure 23: OpenDNS FamilyShield

If you'd prefer to customize settings yourself, click on "Sign up now" for the free OpenDNS Home (*Figure 24*). Start with the free service. You can upgrade to the paid service anytime.

Figure 24: OpenDNS Home

Figure 25 shows the form that you will have to complete.

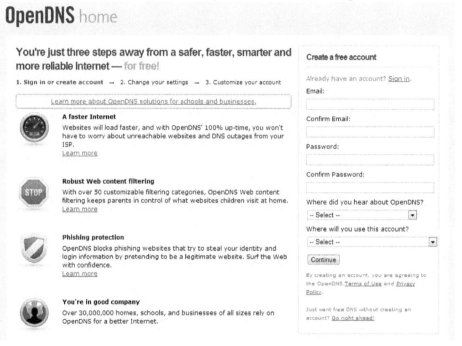

Figure 25: OpenDNS Sign Up Form

For instructions on how to set up your router, select "Router". Note: you will need to know what brand of router you own (*Figure 26*).

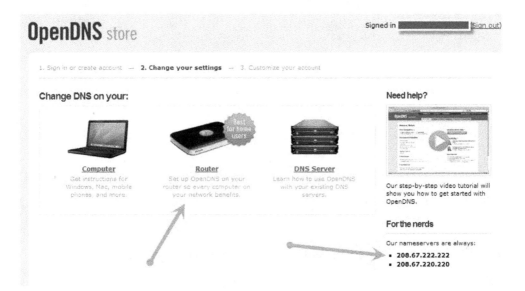

Figure 26: OpenDNS Router Selection

Likely your router will be one of those illustrated in *Figure 27*. If you don't see your device, general router instructions are available via a link at the bottom of the menu. There is an example of my router's DNS set up screen in *Figure 20*.

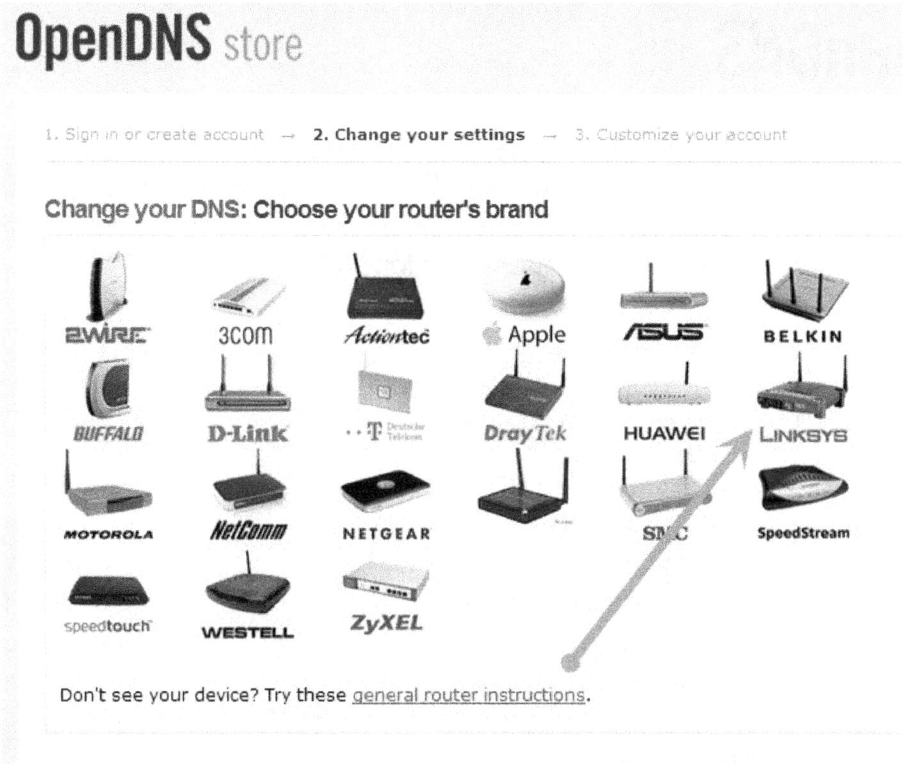

OpenDNS store

1. Sign in or create account → **2. Change your settings** → 3. Customize your account

Change your DNS: Choose your router's brand

2WIRE   3COM   *Actiontec*   Apple   ASUS   BELKIN

BUFFALO   D-Link   T Deutsche Telekom   DrayTek   HUAWEI   LINKSYS

MOTOROLA   NetComm   NETGEAR   SMC   SpeedStream

speedtouch   WESTELL   ZyXEL

Don't see your device? Try these general router instructions.

Figure 27: OpenDNS Router Selection II

Figure 28 includes the instructions that you will need to follow. These particular instructions are for a Linksys E4200, but, regardless of your model, you'll see a similar set up.

OpenDNS store

Change your settings: Configuration for E4200

1. Access the router's browser-based utility.
2. Go to the "Setup" menu.
3. Go to the "Basic Setup" page.
4. Enter the first DNS resolver.
5. Enter the second DNS resolver.
6. Save your settings.

1. Access the router's browser-based utility.

Log into your router's browser-based utility by entering 192.168.1.1 into a br
you are not using Cisco Connect.

2. Go to the "Setup" menu.

Click on the "Setup" tab.

3. Go to the "Basic Setup" page.

Click the "Basic Setup" page.

4. Enter the first DNS resolver.

Enter 208.67.222.222 in the "Static DNS 1" field.

5. Enter the second DNS resolver.

Enter 208.67.220.220 in the "Static DNS 2" field.

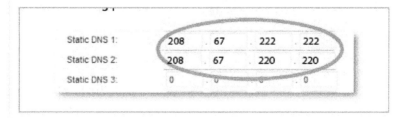

Figure 28: OpenDNS Router Instructions

Test your network by clicking on the "Test your new settings" link (*Figure 29*).

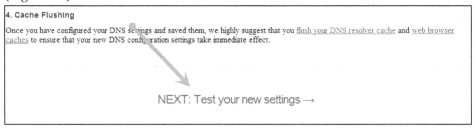

Figure 29: OpenDNS Router Test Page

And whoohoo! We have success (*Figure 30*)! That was the basics. You're almost done.

Figure 30: OpenDNS Success Message

After you open your personal dashboard by clicking on "OpenDNS Dashboard", you can set the protection level that you want to use for your whole home by selecting the "settings" tab (*Figure 31*).

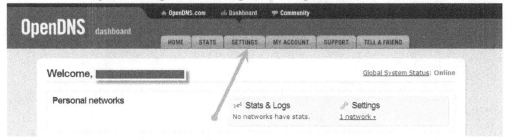

Figure 31: OpenDNS Settings

Select your network (*Figure 32*). In *Figure 32* you can see that mine was "Cox Home".

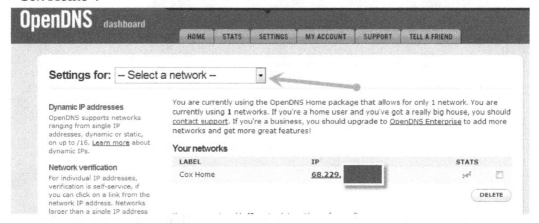

Figure 32: OpenDNS Network Selection

Set your protection level by selecting the radio button and pressing "Apply" (*Figure 33*).

Figure 33: OpenDNS Filter Level

Select the "Security" section on the left and check all three options (Enable basic malware/botnet protection; enable phishing protection; and block internal IP addresses, as in *Figure 34*).

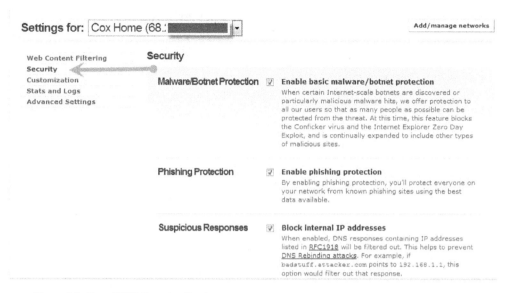

Figure 34: OpenDNS Security Settings

In "Customization" you can put in your own message to your family about why they have been blocked, like "Son, you have been blocked from this site because the computer has determined you are trying to look at naked ladies again" (or use the default like I do - they don't get as cranky!).

Figure 35: OpenDNS Customizations

Your final step is in "Stats and Logs". Check "Enable stats and logs" (*Figure 36*).

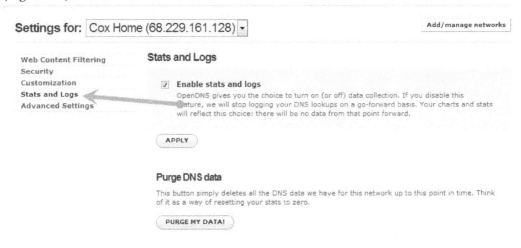

Figure 36: OpenDNS Stats and Logs

This is a very important setting. Enabling stats and logs lets you, as the parent, visit the OpenDNS website and look at your stats (*Figure 37*). You can click on the menu options on the left side and review where people at your house have browsed, sites that have been blocked, and lots of other information about the type of web traffic your family is generating. This information will arm you to talk to you children about their browsing behavior, even if they are trying to hide their browsing from you!

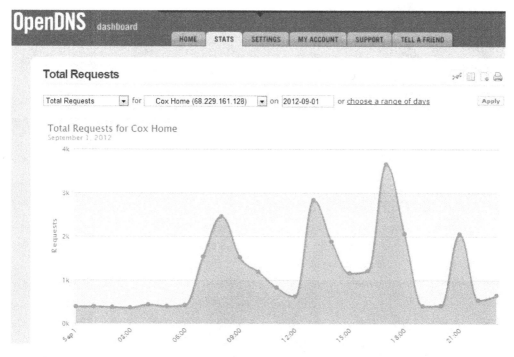

Figure 37: OpenDNS Statistics

And that is it. You are now running OpenDNS at your house, and no one can break the rules without manually selecting their own DNS entry on their computer. Since you've chosen an inscrutable passphrase and kept it secret, no one but you is going to be able to access those manual settings.

By the way, if your child is computer savvy, you should check to see if he/she has changed their network settings on their personal computer and chosen a different DNS address. This is not something most people know how to do, but a determined kid could change these settings.

Configuration for a Parent's Computer Using MS Windows

Set a Computer Password

To set a password for the computer, begin at the Start Menu and click "Control Panel" on the menu on the right. Figure 38 *illustrates this process.*

Figure 38: Start Menu

Windows 8.1 lets you access the control panel in two ways. Right click the Windows menu flag on the desktop (soon to be the menu button again in Windows 10, yay!), then select "Control Panel" *(see Figure 38)*. Another method to reach the control panel is to move the mouse to the upper right, which should trigger the menu to appear on the right side of the screen. Clicking on the symbol of the gear opens the settings menu, from which you can select "Control Panel".

Select "User Accounts and Family Safety" (*Figure 39*), and then "User Accounts" (*Figure 40*).

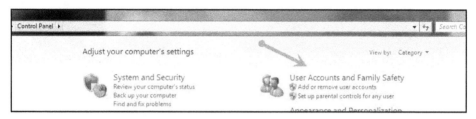

Figure 39: Control Panel

Figure 40: User Accounts

Select "Create a password for your account" (*Figure 41*). If your computer already has a password, "Change your password" will appear instead of this option.

Figure 41. Create a password

Figure 42 shows the password screen. My computer has a password, so a "Current Password" box shows. Without a password your computer will only have the boxes marked by the orange arrows.

Type in a strong password in "New Password" and retype it in "Confirm New Password". Do not forget this password. This is your only access to your computer.

Figure 42: Password Entry

To protect yourself from a forgotten password click on "Create a Password Reset Disk" on the left-hand column and follow the instructions to create this disk (*Figure 43*). Store it in a safe place away from the computer. With this disk you can still get into your computer should you forget the password you just set, but with this disk, anyone can break into your computer. Hide it well!

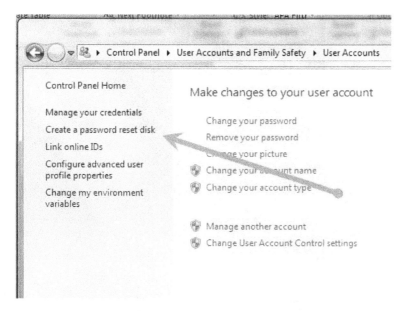

Figure 43: Password Reset Disk

Set Your Screen Saver to Lock

You want to set your screen saver to lock the computer in case you walk away. This prevents anyone else from gaining access to the computer while it is powered on and you are not at it. If you have kids, you will want to set this on your "adult" computer to keep them from using your machine to circumvent all of the protections you have installed on the children's machines.

To set your screen saver to lock, return to the Start Menu and select Control Panel. (*Figure 44*).

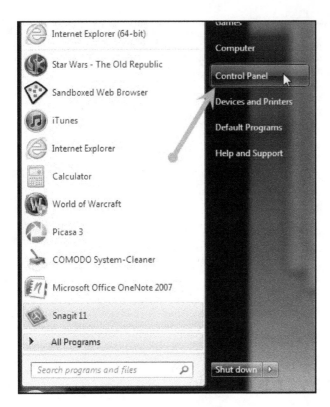

Figure 44. Start Menu

Within the control panel select "Appearance and Personalization" (*Figure 45*).

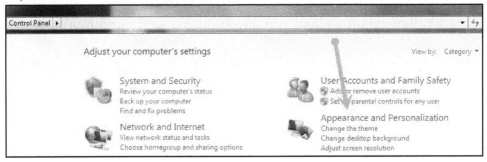

Figure 45: Appearance and Personalization

Now select "Change screen saver" (*Figure 46*).

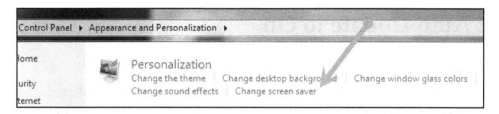

Figure 46: Change Screen Saver

On the screen saver menu, choose your screen saver, set the lock time (I set mine to somewhere around 15 minutes), and choose the box that says "On resume, display logon screen" (*Figure 47*).

Figure 47: Screen Saver

Once you click "Apply", your screen saver is set so when someone jiggles the mouse or tries to use the keyboard, they will have to enter your password before they can continue using your computer.

Set Auto Update to On

To keep your system protected to the best level that Microsoft offers (which is pretty good), set your system to download and install patches from Microsoft when Microsoft releases them. Once again, we are going to access the Control Panel via the Start Menu (*Figure 48*). Select "Control Panel" from the start menu.

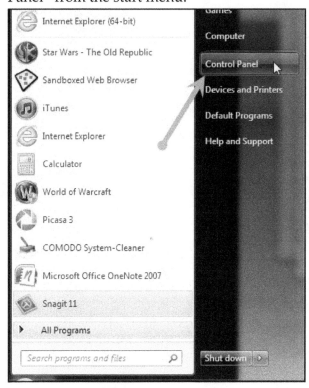

Figure 48: Accessing the Control Panel via the Start Menu

At the control panel you will select "System and Security" (*Figure 49*).

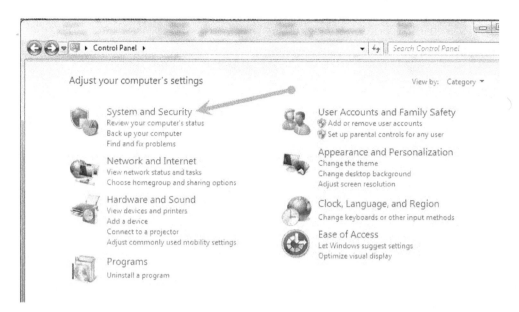

Figure 49: Control Panel - System and Security

Select "Turn automatic updating on or off" (*Figure 50*).

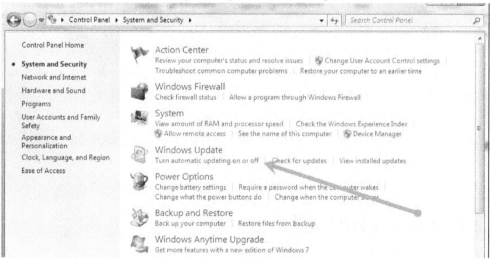

Figure 50: Windows Update

Set the time to "Every day" and pick a time to schedule your updates. Check all four boxes (*Figure 51*).

1. Recommended Updates – Checked
2. Who can install Updates – All users

3. Microsoft Update – Checked
4. Software Notification – Checked

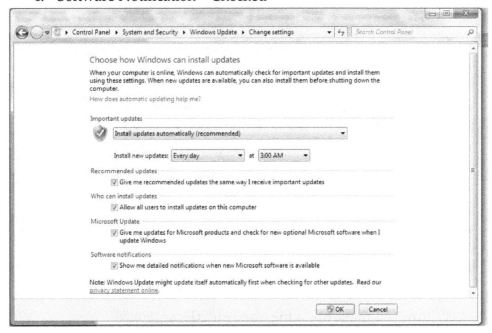

Figure 51: Auto Update Menu

The four boxes in *Figure 51* tell your system to:

- deliver not only important updates, but also recommended updates;
- allow all users to install updates;
- update you on all Microsoft products; and
- display detailed notifications when Microsoft has a new software product related to your computer.

Computer Firewall

Check to Make Sure your Firewall is On

How do you know that your firewall is working? After you install your Internet Security Suite, you will want to make sure that Microsoft sees that it has taken over the firewall duties correctly.

Okay, last time. Really! From the "Start Menu" choose "Control Panel" (*Figure 52*).

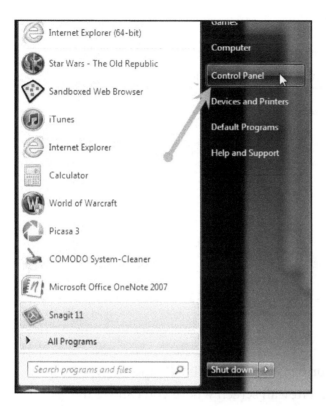

Figure 52: Start Menu

From the control panel choose "System and Security" (*Figure 53*).

Figure 53: Control Panel

When you get to the System and Security menu, about midway down you will see "Windows Firewall" (*Figure 54*). Select this.

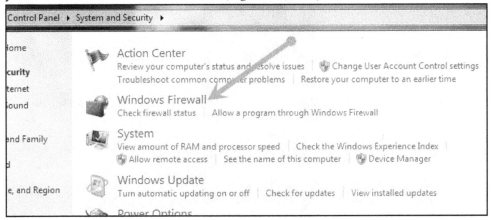

Figure 54: Windows Firewall

On my computer I use Norton 360 as my antivirus and firewall package. *Figure 55* shows the Windows Firewall screen where you can see the message "These settings are being managed by vendor application Norton 360". This is good. This means that Norton was installed correctly and that Windows recognizes that it is running and acting as your firewall on this computer.

Figure 55: Windows Firewall - On

Configuration for a Child's Computer Using MS Windows

To create an account for each child, return to the "Start Menu" and select the "Control Panel" (*Figure 56*).

Figure 56: Start Menu

Select "User Accounts and Family Safety" (*Figure 57*).

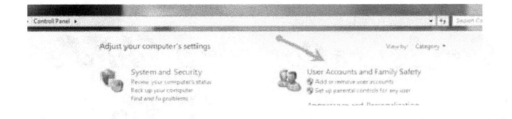

Figure 57: User Accounts and Family Safety

Then select "Add or remove users accounts" (*Figure 58*).

Figure 58: Add or remove user accounts

This will move you to the "Manage Accounts" menu (*Figure 59*). Select "Create a new account".

6

Figure 59: Manage Accounts

Enter the name of the account and leave it as a "Standard User" (*Figure 60*). Click "Create Account".

As standard users, your kids will need to have you input your administrator password if they want to install programs. This is good. Before you enter your password, take a look at what they are installing. Is it from a suspicious source? Is it age-appropriate? Is it something that contributes to your child's highest good, or is it a major waste of their time?

Figure 60: Add new account

Once the account is created, you will be returned to the "Manage Accounts" screen, now reflecting the new account. In *Figure 61,* I called my new standard user "Testaccount". Click on your new account.

Figure 61. Manage Accounts

Click "Create a password" *(Figure 62).* Put in a password for your child. Repeat this account creation process for each child.

Make changes to Testaccount's account

Change the account name

Create a password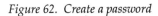

Change the picture

Set up Parental Controls

Change the account type

Delete the account

Manage another account

Testaccount
Standard user

Figure 62. Create a password

Web of Trust (WOT) Sample Set Up

Installing WOT in Chrome™

To add WOT to your Chrome™ browser, click (1) "Wrench", (2) "Tools", then (3) "Extensions" (*Figure 63*).

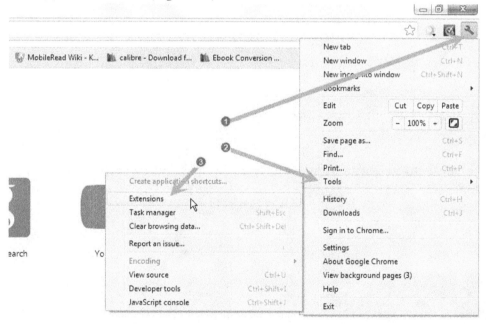

Figure 63: Chrome, the Wrench and Tools menu

This will open a web page. At the bottom of the page (*Figure 64*), click "Get more extensions".

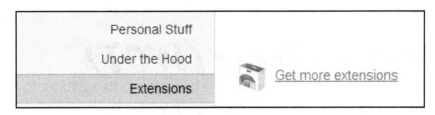

Figure 64: Chrome "Get more extensions" link

Search for WOT (*Figure 65*).

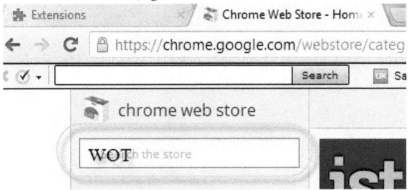

Figure 65: Chrome Extension Search for WOT

Select "Add to Chrome™ next to WOT in the search results (*Figure 66*).

Figure 66: Add to Chrome

Below (*Figure 67*), you will see that I have enabled WOT on my Chrome™ browser.

Figure 67: WOT Extension installed

Installing WOT in Firefox™

To enable WOT in Firefox™, head to the Firefox™ start menu and click the "Add-ons" button (*Figure 68*).

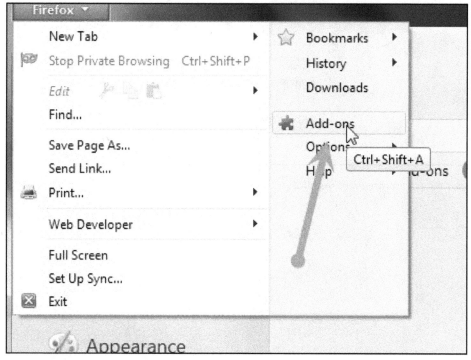

Figure 68: Firefox - Adding Add-Ons

This launches the Add-On Manager. In the search bar on the upper right, type 'WOT' and press enter. Click "Install" next to WOT.

This is the same process for getting any new add-ons: choose the "Get Add-ons" menu and search for them. Below in *Figure 69*, you can see that I have Ad Block Plus, Better Privacy, WOT, and NoScript running on my Firefox™.

Figure 69: Firefox extensions installed

Browser Sample Security Settings

Firefox™ – Mozilla Sample Security Settings

To configure Mozilla's Firefox™, start by pulling down the tool bar under the Firefox™ logo in the upper left corner of the screen. This may seem redundant, but selection "Options" from the "Options" Menu (*Figure 70*).

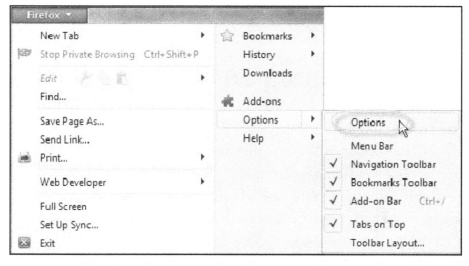

Figure 70: Firefox Options Menu

Click the Privacy Tab within the Options menu. Check "I do not want to be tracked" and set the pull-down to "Never remember history" (*Figure 71*). Remember, on your adult computer you will set it to "Never remember history", but on your child's computer you will set it to "Remember history" (because you want to review that history regularly).

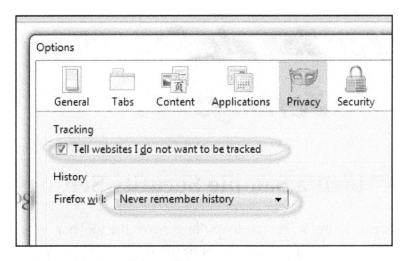

Figure 71: Firefox Privacy Tab

Figure 72 shows the options under the Security Tab. Select:

- "Warn me when a site tries to install add-ons";
- "Block reported attack sites";
- "Block reported web forgeries"; and,
- to ensure passwords do their job to keep people out, **uncheck** both password options:
    - ○ Remember passwords for sites; and
    - ○ Use a master password.

Here we run into that "safety" versus "convenience" problem that plagues security in both the corporate and home arenas. As a parent you wonder, "Why wouldn't I want my child's computer to just plug in the password to Webkinz™?" The answer is if you tell the browser to "Remember passwords for sites," it will remember passwords for ALL sites. Ultimately, it is safer to make your children type the password.

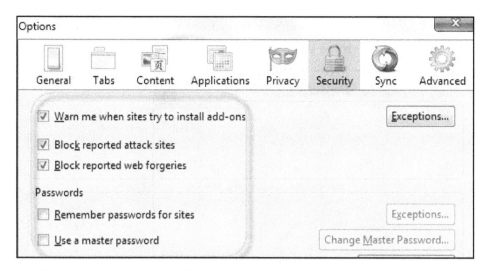

Figure 72: Firefox Security Tab

On the Content tab you will select "Block pop-ups" (*Figure 73*). The other two options are automatically checked, so you can just leave them checked.

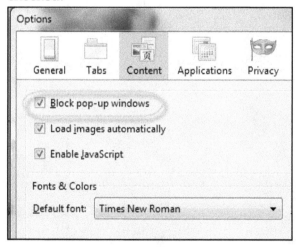

Figure 73: Firefox Content Tab

You now have the basic settings for Firefox. There is still more that you can do to increase your security. You can also install NoScript, Ad Block Plus, Better Privacy, and WOT add-ons. More about these additions is in *Web of Trust Sample Set-Up*.

When you have added your extensions to Firefox your extensions menu will look something like mine below, with Adblock, Better Privacy, Element Hiding Helper, WOT, and NoScript (*Figure 74*).

Figure 74: Firefox extensions installed

Chrome™ – Google Sample Security Settings

Here are the basic security settings for Chrome™. Start by clicking on the wrench in the upper right corner.

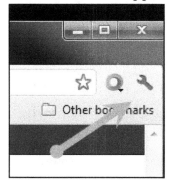

Figure 75: Chrome the "wrench"

Next, select "Settings" (*Figure 76*).

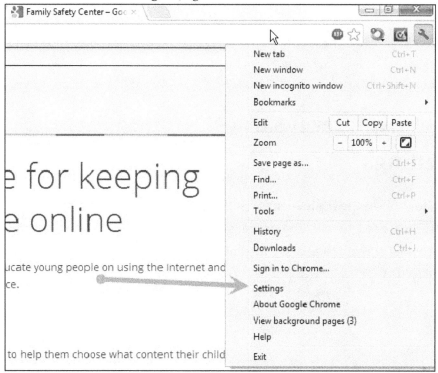

Figure 76. Chrome Settings

Chrome™ will open a new tab that looks like a web page. There will be four options flowing down the left bar. To safeguard your passwords, select "Personal Stuff" and check "Never Save Passwords" (*Figure 77*).

Chrome™ is preconfigured with good security settings, so I don't change any other settings.

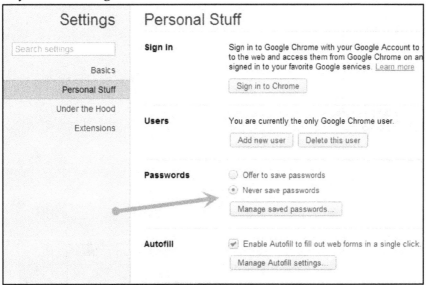

Figure 77: Chrome Personal Stuff Menu

Internet Explorer (v8 or v9) Sample Security Settings

Here's how to set the basic security settings in Microsoft's Internet Explorer (IE) v9. Start by clicking on the gear in the upper right hand corner of the IE Browser screen, to access "Internet options" (*Figure 78*).

Figure 78: Internet Explorer (IE)

This will present you with the Internet Options pop-up screen (*Figure 79*). On the "General" tab, check "Delete Browsing History on Exit" (circled in *Figure 79*).

Figure 79: IE Internet Options

To discourage websites from tracking your usage, move to the Privacy Tab (*Figure 80*) and check "Never allow websites to request your physical location". This is also where you can block pop ups by checking "Turn on Pop-up Blocker" (or if you prefer to block pop-ups on a case by case basis, manually turn back on pop ups). Now set the slider to Medium or higher.

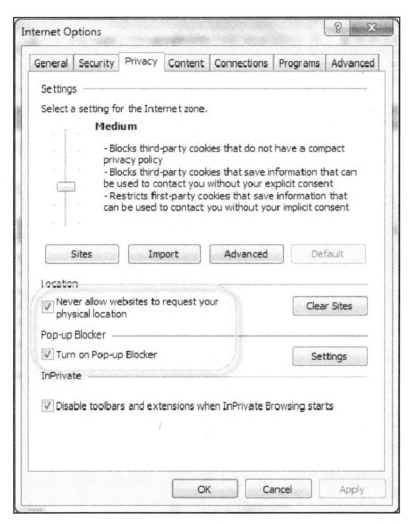

Figure 80: IE Internet Options "Privacy Tab"

Locking Google Safe Search Mode

Follow these steps to lock Google Safe Search:

- Visit the Search settings page (www.google.com/preferences), drag the slider to "Strict", and click "Lock Safe Search" (*Figure 81*).
- If you're not signed in to your Google Account, you'll be prompted to sign in. (Don't have a Google Account? You can create one for free.)
- Once you've signed in and clicked Lock Safe Search (this step takes a moment, because strict filtering is being applied to all Google domains), safe searching will be set and locked on this computer until you use your password to remove it.

You'll see a confirmation page once the lock is engaged.

Figure 81: Google Search Preferences

Google SSL Sample Settings

To set Google SSL in Chrome™, open the "Settings" under the little wrench on the upper right of the browser main menu bar (*Figure 82*).

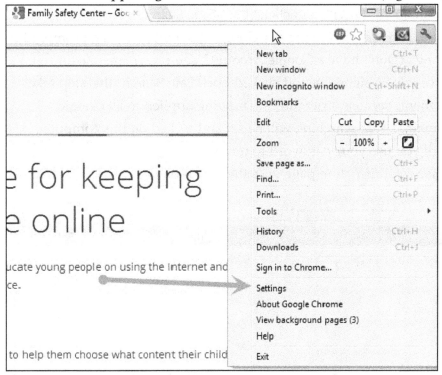

Figure 82: Setting Google SSL in Chrome

The "Settings" page will open. Select "Manage search engines" (*Figure 83*).

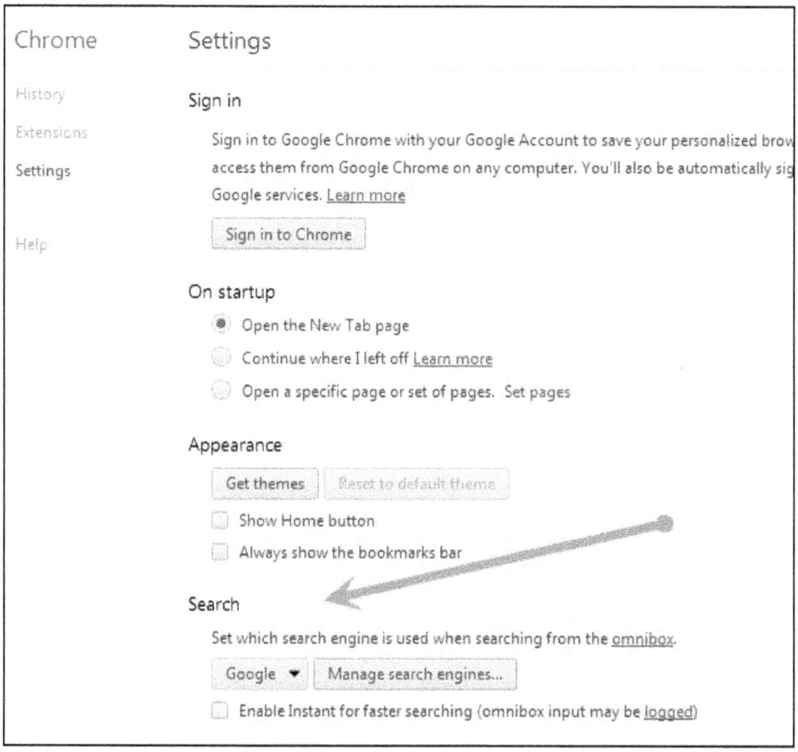

Figure 83: Chrome Manage Search Engines

In the "Add a new search engine" box, under "Other Search Engines" (*Figure 84*), give your new search engine a name. I use "Google SSL" and a keyword like "SSLG". Type the following into the URL box: https://encrypted.google.com/searchq=%s (*Figure 84*).

Figure 84: Chrome Other Search Engine

Your new search engine should be filled in like *Figure 85* (except, of course, with your own search engine name and key word).

Figure 85: Chrome with new search engine

After you've completed the boxes and clicked "OK", a box will appear so you can click "Make Default", to choose your default search engine.

Social Media Account Suggestions

Facebook and Social Media Accounts

Social media sites like Facebook, Tumblr, and YouTube change their settings frequently, partially to offer more protections and partially because some are hoping you will not block some settings. You may recall that many social media sites sell your information unless you specifically tell them not to. My advice here is to set every possible block, lock, protection, and filter that you can live with. You do not want to be publically searchable, so turn that setting off. You do not want to have everything you say or post go to every user, only to your friends and followers. Before you use a service, dig around in the settings for "Security" or "Privacy" and set them appropriately. Search the Internet for phrases like "Privacy on Facebook" or "Privacy settings on Facebook" and read what others have found. Finally, stay on top of their changes. Every time they announce an improvement or version, learn what it does and see if you need to change your settings.

Twitter Account Suggestions

These are the settings I use in my Twitter account. First and foremost, always log on to Twitter using HTTPS.

Figure 86: Twitter HTTPS

To access the settings in Twitter click on the little person in the upper right corner of the screen and select "Settings" (*Figure 87*).

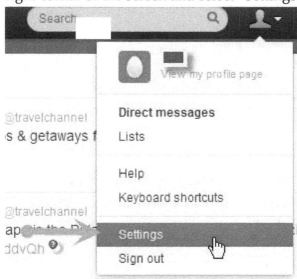

Figure 87: Twitter Settings Menu

In "Account Settings" do not check "Add a location to my tweets". There is no need for everyone on Twitter to see where you are when you tweet. Do not check either of the options under "Tweet Media":

- Do not "Display media that may contain sensitive content.

- Do not "Mark my media as containing sensitive content.

Check the box marked "Protect My Tweets" (*Figure 88*).

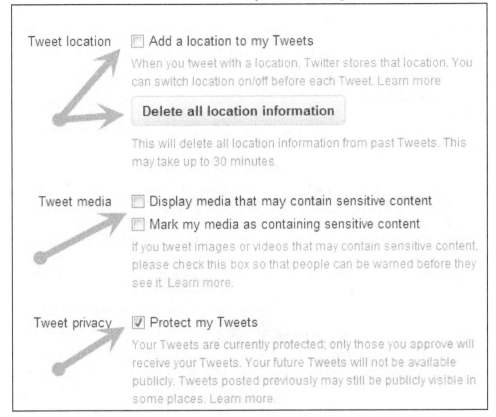

Figure 88: Twitter Account Settings (1)

Check "Always use HTTPS" so you will always use the encrypted version of Twitter. Also check "Require personal information to reset my password", as this is the safer method to reset your password should you forget it.

HTTPS only ☑ Always use HTTPS
Use a secure connection where possible.

Password reset ☑ Require personal information to reset my password
By default, you can initiate a password reset by entering only your @username. If you check this box, you will be prompted to enter your email address or phone number if you forget your password.

Country United States ▼
Select your country. This setting is saved to this browser.

Save changes

Figure 89: Twitter Account Settings (2)

Under "Mobile", just as in Facebook, I do not put in a phone number.

In the "Notification" menu, I check everything on the page. I want to know when someone tweets me, or re-tweets, or follows me (*Figure 90*).

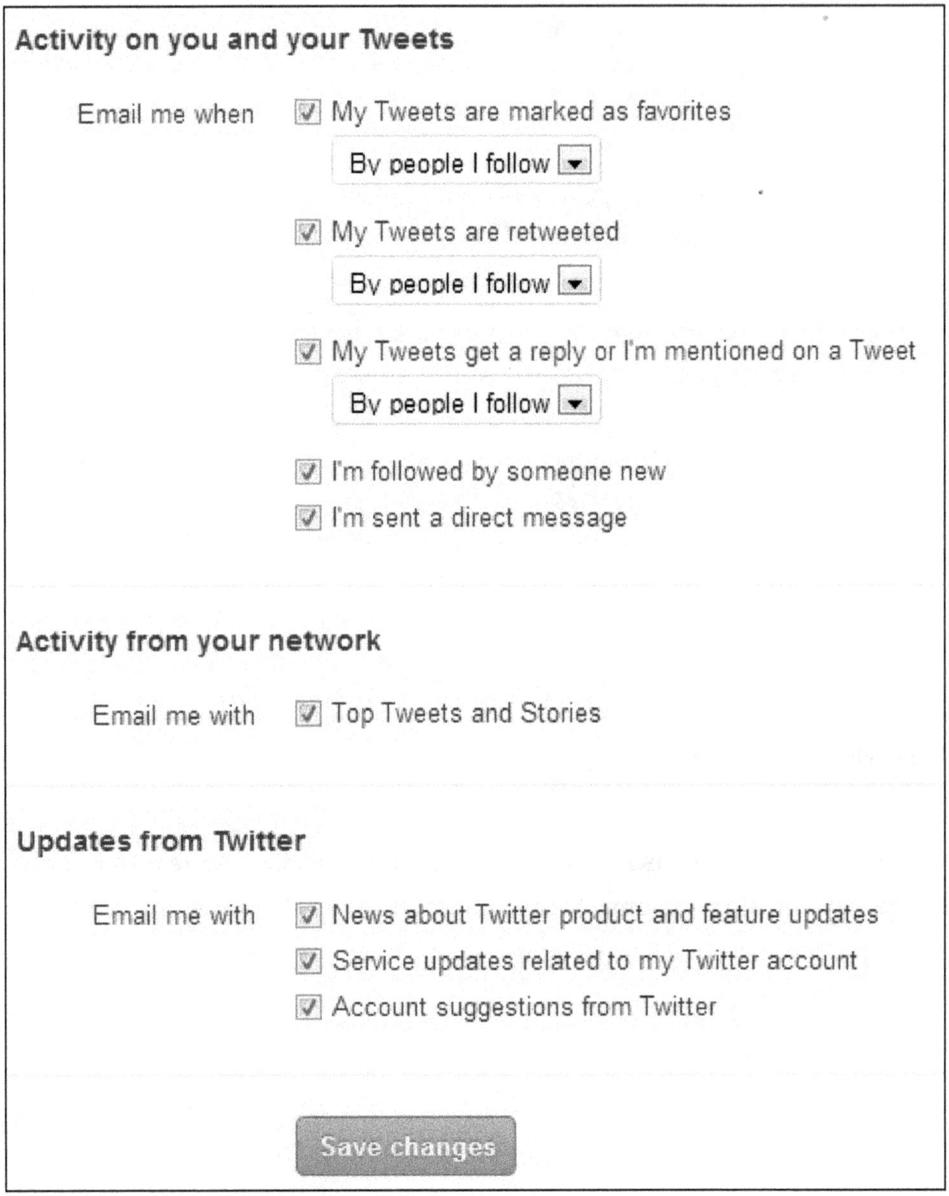

Activity on you and your Tweets

Email me when   ☑ My Tweets are marked as favorites

By people I follow ▼

☑ My Tweets are retweeted

By people I follow ▼

☑ My Tweets get a reply or I'm mentioned on a Tweet

By people I follow ▼

☑ I'm followed by someone new
☑ I'm sent a direct message

Activity from your network

Email me with   ☑ Top Tweets and Stories

Updates from Twitter

Email me with   ☑ News about Twitter product and feature updates
☑ Service updates related to my Twitter account
☑ Account suggestions from Twitter

Save changes

Figure 90: Twitter Notifications

Browser History Review

Reviewing Browser History in Internet Explorer™

To review the browser history in Microsoft Internet Explorer™ click on the "Star" (*Figure 91*). This lowers a menu on which you click the "History" tab. On this tab you can review the websites that have been visited.

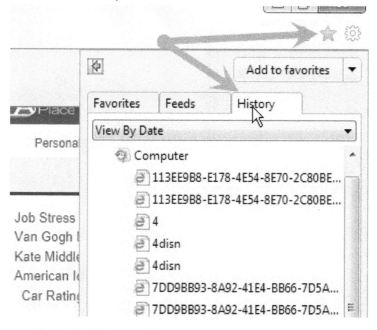

Figure 91: IE Browser History

Reviewing Browser History in Chrome™

To review the browser history in Chrome™ click on the "Three Bars" (*Figure 92*). This lowers a menu on which you click the "History"

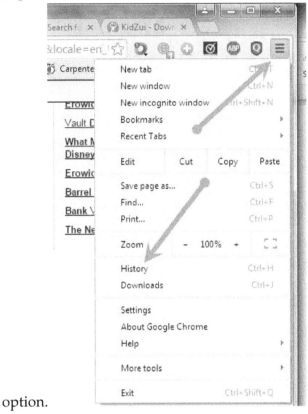

option.

Figure 92: Chrome Wrench - History

On the "History" tab you can review the websites that have been visited (*Figure 93*).

Figure 93: Chrome History

Reviewing Browser History in Firefox™

To review the browser history in Firefox™ click on the "Firefox" menu, then "History", and "Show All History" (*Figure 94*).

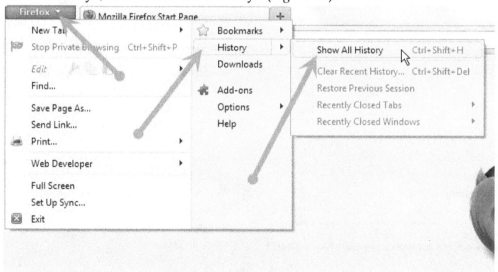

Figure 94: Firefox History

Index

credit card, 28, 50, 55, 56, 58, 59, 60, 63, 64, 65, 68, 72, 80, 83, 130

cyber harassment, 24

cyberbullying, 20, 24, 25, 35, 44

D

debit card, 60

Disney, 28, 29, 44, 51, 59, 204, 205

Disneyland, 204

DNS, 39, 110, 115, 116, 126, 141, 147, 148, 149, 150, 152, 159

DNS resolution, 39, 116

download, 67, 71, 72, 137

driving, 100

Dropbox, 62

E

email, 18, 19, 21, 24, 25, 31, 32, 33, 34, 36, 37, 42, 45, 50, 62, 65, 67, 68, 69, 76, 77, 78, 79, 80, 81, 83, 91, 94, 98, 102, 104, 114, 137

encryption, 52, 62, 101, 120

Epic Browser, 132

Evernote, 62

excessive gaming, 29

eye rolling, 32

F

Facebook, 11, 21, 23, 24, 26, 35, 36, 38, 42, 44, 45, 50, 51, 54, 56, 84, 85, 88, 89, 90, 91, 92, 93, 97, 98, 105, 126, 142, 192, 195

FaceTime, 117

file sharing, 71, 72

filter, 20, 38, 81, 105

Firefox, 35, 59, 131, 132, 133, 136, 142, 177, 178, 179, 180, 181, 182, 199

firewall, 14, 56, 57, 58, 75, 111, 112, 113, 114, 120, 121, 124, 138, 141, 143, 168, 170

fraud, 69

friended, 23, 85

G

games, 17, 26, 27, 28, 29, 40, 56, 57, 104, 127, 135

gaming console, 19

geeks, 131

Google+, 25, 45, 85, 88, 94

googling, 19

guinea pig, 11, 12, 49

H

hacker, 68, 69, 72, 73, 90, 91, 110, 112, 124, 134

house rules, 17, 41, 42

HTTPS, 58, 59, 93, 130, 193, 194

I

Ice Dragon, 133

iCloud, 62

identity theft, 20

images, 25, 78, 80, 97, 137

Immunet, 58, 75, 121, 123, 124

Instagram, 34

Internet Explorer, 35, 58, 132, 184, 185, 197

Internet safety, 13, 16

K

K9, 22, 38, 116, 127, 128, 138, 139, 142

KeePass, 52

kids' browsers, 9, 136

L

laptop, 14, 22, 32, 52, 100, 101, 102, 103, 117, 119, 129, 142, 143

link scanner, 135

Linksys, 39, 112, 119, 153

logging, 114, 116, 141

About the Author

Kevin Russell grew up a stone's throw from Disneyland, playing tour guide for every Midwestern relative that came to visit. Now a Midwesterner himself, Kevin has discovered the Happiest Place on Earth on the other coast: Walt Disney World. After being plied with too many lunches from friends asking for Disney vacation advice, Kevin started collecting his tips in notes that eventually, with the help of his wife, evolved into *Dads (& Mom's) Disney Do's & Don'ts*. When he and his family are not at Walt Disney World, Kevin can be found planning their next Walt Disney World trip and saving the world, one information security crisis at a time. Ok. Sometimes two. When he grows up, Kevin hopes to be a Monorail pilot.

Thank you for purchasing this book. If you have enjoyed it, found it useful, or it touched your life in some small way, please consider posting a review on www.amazon.com and/or Barnes & Noble (www.bn.com). You can contact Kevin directly with your ideas, suggestions, or experiences at author@dadsdosanddonts.com.

Look for *Dad's (& Mom's) Disney Do's and Don'ts*, 2015 edition, coming 2015, for practical advice on your family's next trip to Disney World.

www.ingramcontent.com/pod-product-compliance
Lightning Source LLC
Chambersburg PA
CBHW080410060326
40689CB00019B/4199